Teaching Assistant Training in the 1990s

Jody D. Nyquist, Robert D. Abbott,
Donald H. Wulff, *Editors*
University of Washington

NEW DIRECTIONS FOR TEACHING AND LEARNING
ROBERT E. YOUNG, *Editor-in-Chief*
University of Wisconsin

Number 39, Fall 1989

Paperback sourcebooks in
The Jossey-Bass Higher Education Series

Jossey-Bass Inc., Publishers
San Francisco • Oxford

Jody D. Nyquist, Robert D. Abbott, Donald H. Wulff (eds.).
Teaching Assistant Training in the 1990s.
New Directions for Teaching and Learning, no. 39.
San Francisco: Jossey-Bass, 1989.

New Directions for Teaching and Learning
Robert E. Young, *Editor-in-Chief*

Copyright © 1989 by Jossey-Bass Inc., Publishers

Copyright under International, Pan American, and Universal
Copyright Conventions. All rights reserved. No part of
this issue may be reproduced in any form—except for brief
quotation (not to exceed 500 words) in a review or professional
work—without permission in writing from the publishers.

New Directions for Teaching and Learning is published quarterly
by Jossey-Bass Inc., Publishers, 350 Sansome Street, San Francisco,
California, 94104. Second-class postage rates paid at San Francisco,
California, and at additional mailing offices. POSTMASTER: Send
address changes to *New Directions for Teaching and Learning*,
Jossey-Bass Inc., Publishers, 350 Sansome Street, San Francisco,
California 94104.

Editorial correspondence should be sent to the Editor-in-Chief,
Robert E. Young, Dean, University of Wisconsin Center, Fox Valley,
1478 Midway Rd., Menasha, Wisconsin 54952.

Library of Congress Catalog Card Number LC 85-644763
International Standard Serial Number ISSN 0271-0633
International Standard Book Number ISBN 1-55542-858-4

Cover art by WILLI BAUM
Manufactured in the United States of America. Printed on acid-free paper.

Ordering Information

The paperback sourcebooks listed below are published quarterly and can be ordered either by subscription or single copy.

Subscriptions cost $56.00 per year for institutions, agencies, and libraries. Individuals can subscribe at the special rate of $42.00 per year *if payment is by personal check.* (Note that the full rate of $56.00 applies if payment is by institutional check, even if the subscription is designated for an individual.) Standing orders are accepted.

Single copies are available at $12.95 when payment accompanies order. (California, New Jersey, New York, and Washington, D.C., residents please include appropriate sales tax.) For billed orders, cost per copy is $12.95 plus postage and handling.

Substantial discounts are offered to organizations and individuals wishing to purchase bulk quantities of Jossey-Bass sourcebooks. Please inquire.

Please note that these prices are for the calendar year 1989 and are subject to change without notice. Also, some titles may be out of print and therefore not available for sale.

To ensure correct and prompt delivery, all orders must give either the *name of an individual* or an *official purchase order number.* Please submit your order as follows:

Subscriptions: specify series and year subscription is to begin.
Single Copies: specify sourcebook code (such as, TL1) and first two words of title.

Mail all orders to:
 Jossey-Bass Inc., Publishers
 350 Sansome Street
 San Francisco, California 94104

New Directions for Teaching and Learning Series
Robert E. Young, *Editor-in-Chief*

TL1 *Improving Teaching Styles,* Kenneth E. Eble
TL2 *Learning, Cognition, and College Teaching,* Wilbert J. McKeachie
TL3 *Fostering Critical Thinking,* Robert E. Young
TL4 *Learning About Teaching,* John F. Noonan

TL5	*The Administrator's Role in Effective Teaching*, Alan E. Guskin
TL6	*Liberal Learning and Careers*, Charles S. Green III, Richard G. Salem
TL7	*New Perspectives on Teaching and Learning*, Warren Bryan Martin
TL8	*Interdisciplinary Teaching*, Alvin M. White
TL9	*Expanding Learning Through New Communications Technologies*, Christopher K. Knapper
TL10	*Motivating Professors to Teach Effectively*, James L. Bess
TL11	*Practices That Improve Teaching Evaluation*, Grace French-Lazovik
TL12	*Teaching Writing in All Disciplines*, C. Williams Griffin
TL13	*Teaching Values and Ethics in College*, Michael J. Collins
TL14	*Learning in Groups*, Clark Bouton, Russell Y. Garth
TL15	*Revitalizing Teaching Through Faculty Development*, Paul A. Lacey
TL16	*Teaching Minority Students*, James H. Cones III, John F. Noonan, Denise Janha
TL17	*The First Year of College Teaching*, L. Dee Fink
TL18	*Increasing the Teaching Role of Academic Libraries*, Thomas G. Kirk
TL19	*Teaching and Aging*, Chandra M. N. Mehrotra
TL20	*Rejuvenating Introductory Courses*, Karen I. Spear
TL21	*Teaching as Though Students Mattered*, Joseph Katz
TL22	*Strengthening the Teaching Assistant Faculty*, John D. W. Andrews
TL23	*Using Research to Improve Teaching*, Janet C. Donald, Arthur M. Sullivan
TL24	*College-School Collaboration: Appraising the Major Approaches*, William T. Daly
TL25	*Fostering Academic Excellence Through Honors Programs*, Paul G. Friedman, Reva Jenkins-Friedman
TL26	*Communicating in College Classrooms*, Jean M. Civikly
TL27	*Improving Teacher Education*, Eva C. Galambos
TL28	*Distinguished Teachers on Effective Teaching*, Peter G. Beidler
TL29	*Coping with Faculty Stress*, Peter Seldin
TL30	*Developing Critical Thinking and Problem-Solving Abilities*, James E. Stice
TL31	*Techniques for Evaluating and Improving Instruction*, Lawrence M. Aleamoni
TL32	*Teaching Large Classes Well*, Maryellen Gleason Weimer
TL33	*College Teaching and Learning: Preparing for New Commitments*, Robert E. Young, Kenneth E. Eble
TL34	*Assessing Students' Learning*, Robert E. Young, Kenneth E. Eble
TL35	*Knowing and Doing: Learning Through Experience*, Pat Hutchings, Allen Wutzdorff
TL36	*Strengthening Programs for Writing Across the Curriculum*, Susan H. McLeod
TL37	*The Department Chairperson's Role in Enhancing College Teaching*, Ann F. Lucas
TL38	*Promoting Inquiry in Undergraduate Learning*, Frederick Stirton Weaver

Contents

Editors' Notes 1
Jody D. Nyquist, Robert D. Abbott, Donald H. Wulff

Part 1. The Context of TA Training

1. The Challenge of TA Training in the 1990s 7
Jody D. Nyquist, Robert D. Abbott, Donald H. Wulff
The context in which TA training takes place today has changed from what it was in past decades. Yet many of the questions about training TAs remain unresolved. In this chapter, the authors discuss the present status of TA training and suggest a conceptualization for thinking about TA training in the 1990s.

2. Socialization of Teaching Assistants 15
Ann Q. Staton, Ann L. Darling
Socialization occurs through a process of communication as TAs learn what it means to be teachers as well as graduate students. This chapter discusses specific ways in which TAs are socialized into their teaching roles.

3. Teaching in a Diverse Environment: Knowledge and Skills Needed by TAs 23
Nancy Van Note Chism, Jamie Cano, Anne S. Pruitt
An increasingly diverse student body requires that faculty of the future develop specific sensitivities and a broader range of teaching strategies to use with students. This chapter focuses on issues and strategies related to diversity based on age, disability, gender, cultural and ethnic backgrounds, and sexual orientation.

4. TA Supervision 37
Jo Sprague, Jody D. Nyquist
Often a TA's success depends on an effective relationship with a supervisor. In this chapter, the authors propose a developmental perspective as a way for supervisors to work with TAs.

Part 2. Current Training Programs

5. Designing Programs to Prepare TAs to Teach 57
Maryellen Weimer, Marilla D. Svinicki, Gabriele Bauer
The design of TA training programs requires the consideration of several basic questions. This chapter addresses some of these questions by presenting the results of a survey of fourteen institutions that are actively involved in TA training.

6. ITA Training Programs 71
Janet C. Constantinides
Programs for international teaching assistants are varied. In this chapter, the author describes four different types of programs and suggests that staffing is a key element.

7. Issues in ITA Training Programs 79
Debra-L Sequeira, Magdalena Costantino
Successful development of programs for international teaching assistants requires consideration of a variety of issues. The authors of this chapter identify and discuss contemporary dilemmas that face those involved in ITA training programs.

Part 3. New Directions in TA Training

8. Helping TAs Use Active Learning Strategies 89
Deborah H. Hatch, Christine R. Farris
TAs can use writing and collaboration as active learning strategies in their classrooms. In this chapter, the authors use case examples to suggest that training TAs to use active learning strategies may involve a wider range of issues than might be apparent initially.

9. Classroom Research for Teaching Assistants 99
Thomas A. Angelo, K. Patricia Cross
Classroom research is one way for TAs to obtain data to assist them with their teaching. In this chapter the authors propose turning TAs into classroom researchers to improve the effectiveness of higher education.

Part 4. Research and Resources for TA Training

10. Review of Research on TA Training 111
Robert D. Abbott, Donald H. Wulff, C. Kati Szego
The development of TA training programs can benefit from relevant research. The authors of this chapter examine the research on TA training, discuss its implications for TA training programs, and suggest directions for future research.

11. TA Training Resources 125
Delivee L. Wright
An important part of the development of successful TA training programs is the use of appropriate resources. This chapter provides a selected list of resources useful for TA training, including print materials, videotapes, and guides for program development.

Index 133

Editors' Notes

Calls for better training of our nation's teaching assistants (TAs) have remained unchanged over the last sixty years. Meanwhile, the issues surrounding TA training have become increasingly complicated. Confronting the lack of adequate training, sorting out the complexity of the contexts in which TAs work, and identifying obstacles to adequate TA training have become tasks that must engage TAs, TA supervisors, faculty, instructional developers, department chairs, deans, and graduate school administrators.

Even in institutions where attention has been paid to these issues and where decision makers are ready to commit time and money to the effort, the complexity of the enterprise is formidable. We do not have specific answers about what should be provided for all TAs as they prepare to work with undergraduates in the office, lab, or classroom. What should be done depends on the TAs, the students they are dealing with, the types of tasks assigned, the discipline and institutional context of their teaching, and the supervision they are given. The answers do not come easy, and it is often the subtleties of the situation that determine the most promising ways to proceed in designing TA training programs.

The authors of this volume do not claim to have complete answers to the questions surrounding TA training, but they do have experience in working with TAs and have attempted to share their thinking about selected issues. These are issues that we must address if we are to improve the quality of TA training.

Part One describes the pressing demands within which TA training now occurs and the people most directly involved in the context of the TA experience: the TAs themselves, the students they teach, and the supervisors they interact with. Chapter One provides a conceptual basis for thinking about the challenges of TA training in the 1990s. In Chapter Two, on the socialization of teaching assistants, Staton and Darling examine how TAs learn about being a TA. Their finding, that new TAs rely heavily on experienced TAs to learn their roles, has significant implications for the planning of TA training programs. Chapter Three, by Chism, Cano, and Pruitt, addresses issues and strategies related to training TAs to teach diverse groups of students, with particular emphasis on age, disability, gender, sexual orientation, and cultural and ethnic background. Chapter Four addresses the supervisor-TA relationship. Sprague and Nyquist propose that viewing the training of TAs from a developmental perspective will enable supervisors to respond to TAs' needs according to the individual TA's stage of development.

Part Two deals with the status of current training programs across the United States. In Chapter Five, Weimer, Svinicki, and Bauer describe TA training models on the basis of a survey of fourteen institutions actively involved in TA training. Chapter Six, by Constantinides, and Chapter Seven, by Sequeira and Costantino, deal with the complex issues of training international teaching assistants (ITAs). Constantinides describes ITA training programs; Sequeira and Costantino extend this discussion to consider current dilemmas facing developers of ITA training programs.

Part Three responds to the call for TAs to consider undergraduates as active learners and to become more reflective about their teaching as they consider its improvement. In Chapter Eight, Hatch and Farris focus on writing and working collaboratively as examples of active learning that TAs can use in their classrooms. They identify a number of the problems encountered in training TAs to use such strategies. In Chapter Nine, Angelo and Cross present their approach for training teaching assistants to gather data about the effectiveness of their teaching by becoming "classroom researchers."

The two chapters in Part Four identify research and resources that developers of TA training can call upon. In Chapter Ten, Abbott, Wulff, and Szego examine research since 1980 on TA training. They have found little research that examines the effectiveness of many widely used TA training approaches, but they hope that future TA training approaches can be informed by relevant research, and they provide some directions which further research might take. In Chapter Eleven, Wright offers a listing of resources useful for developers of TA training programs.

This volume addresses some of the issues and extends current conceptualizations about the role of the teaching assistant. The authors deal with the experience afforded the individual TA, the importance of the TA role to the teaching of undergraduates and to the recruitment and preparation of tomorrow's professors, and the types of preparation that allow TAs to fulfill their current instructional responsibilities and future professiorial roles. Our hope is that careful examination of these aspects of training programs will lead to further understanding of TAs, their roles, and universities' responsibility to them as the professors of tomorrow.

Jody D. Nyquist
Robert D. Abbott
Donald H. Wulff
Editors

Jody D. Nyquist is a lecturer in the Department of Speech Communication and is director for instructional development at the Center for Instructional Development and Research, University of Washington.

Robert D. Abbott is professor of educational psychology and director for program research at the Center for Instructional Development and Research, University of Washington.

Donald H. Wulff is assistant director of the Center for Instructional Development and Research, University of Washington.

Part 1.

The Context of TA Training

With the development of disciplinary knowledge, greater student diversity, advances in learning theory, and an increased emphasis on undergraduate education, the design of effective TA training must consider the interaction of many dimensions that affect TAs' performance.

The Challenge of TA Training in the 1990s

Jody D. Nyquist, Robert D. Abbott, Donald H. Wulff

As colleges and universities attempt to adequately train teaching assistants (TAs), the complexity of the task has become clear. Responsible for a substantial percentage of undergraduate instruction (Nyquist and Wulff, 1987), teaching assistants are assigned a wide range of duties. TAs conduct quiz sections or laboratories for lecture courses, provide tutorial sessions, grade exams, review tests and answer questions, and hold office hours. In less frequent cases, TAs are given total responsibility for courses, including text selection, assignment of students' work, testing of students' achievement, and final grading of students.

Developing programs that will adequately prepare TAs to assume these responsibilities demands the best thinking of university administrators, graduate school deans, department chairs, college deans, instructional and faculty developers, faculty, and teaching assistants' supervisors. Who is responsible for the training? What training is most appropriate? What can be taught across the disciplines? What must be presented within a discipline? Should TAs be "practicing" on undergraduates? For what purpose(s) are TAs being trained—their present assignments, or their future careers? All these questions stream by in somewhat overwhelming and seemingly unanswered forms. The issues are complicated, and anyone seriously attempting to make thoughtful decisions about TA training cannot help being perplexed.

Contrary to the prevailing view, this is not a new development but only one whose resolution has been long deferred. As early as 1930, at the meetings of the Administrative Officers of Higher Institutions in Chicago, Laing, then Dean of the Graduate School at the University of Chicago, asked a series of questions:

> What are we doing in the way of equipping them [the graduate students] for their chosen work? Have the departments of the various graduate schools kept the teaching career sufficiently in mind in the organization of their program[s] of studies? Or have they arranged their courses with an eye to the production of research workers only, thinking of the teacher's duties merely as a means of livelihood that will furnish the young instructor or professor with enough money to buy food, drink, clothes, and shelter for himself and his family, and enable him to pay insurance premiums and contribute to the portrait funds of retiring colleagues, while he carries on his research? And finally comes the question: What sort of college teachers do our Doctors of Philosophy make? I do not mean to imply that these are all the questions that have been or might be asked, but they are some of the most obvious ones [Laing, 1930, p. 51].

The same issues surfaced again in 1949, at a conference on college teachers' preparation. As in 1930, the conference speakers in 1949 lamented the fact that little was being done to prepare college teachers for their jobs, and they expressed the overwhelming sentiment that the role of the graduate school was to produce learned scholars, in the hope that they might also become accomplished teachers (Wise, 1967). Again in the late 1950s, and once more in the 1960s, conferences were held and calls for reform were made, but little change occurred. The 1980s brought more campuswide TA orientation programs, as well as the publication of Andrews's (1985) volume.

As we approach the 1990s, we continue to consider TA issues, as evidenced by recent presentations at the meetings of the Council of Graduate Schools and the American Association of Higher Education and by the National TA Training conferences of 1986 and 1989. For the most part, however, the emphasis on the graduate school experience is still focused on graduate study and research, and graduate students are provided only limited preparation for the teaching duties they assume. Laing's (1930) questions remain unanswered in 1989, nearly sixty years later.

Added to these unresolved issues is the urgent need to replace the "graying" professoriate. The next ten years will see a mass exodus of the professors hired during the growth years of the 1950s and 1960s. We do not have enough graduate students preparing to become academicians to meet this demand, especially in the sciences. An interesting question of cause and effect arises: Is the professional development of graduate TAs only minimally addressed because they are not choosing academic careers, or are graduate students not choosing academic careers because their experiences as TAs do not adequately prepare them for and entice them into the professoriate? We need not answer these questions to recognize that, although not all TAs are going to be professors, virtually all professors were once TAs.

The Need for Action

Not to take action at this time may have serious consequences. Not to act is to decide that the 500,000 new professors who will be needed by 2014 will probably not be prepared to teach undergraduates. Much has happened to change the scene of American higher education since 1930, and even since 1980. Many of these changes require new ways of teaching new types of students.

First, the accelerated development of knowledge in all disciplines means that introductory courses can no longer focus on transmitting all that is known in a discipline to undergraduates; rather, undergraduates must be able to manage large amounts of changing information at a quickening rate. Learning how to find information and transform it for their own use will be necessary for all students. Learning strategies that worked for professors when they were undergraduates may not longer be sufficient for current undergraduates attempting to acquire the increasingly complex knowledge of a discipline in the short span of four or five years. TAs will need to be able to teach students the most efficient ways of approaching the tasks of learning. TAs who are entering the professoriate will need to acquire the most efficient ways of approaching the tasks of teaching. Knowledge of instructional computing applications for managing various teaching tasks will be a necessity.

Beyond the management of information, TAs must be taught methods for actively engaging students in the practices of a discipline. To help undergraduates become efficient problem solvers in the discipline, TAs must be taught methods that will help undergraduates think as sociologists, as physicists, as chemists, as historians. Information management and problem solving within a discipline provide new and continually changing demands for TAs, the professors of the 1990s.

Second, the university student body of the 1990s will increasingly reflect the diversity of our society (Green, 1988). For the most part, institutions of higher education have ignored this growing diversity, expecting nontraditional students to adjust and conform to prevailing norms, which frequently ignore minority groups. Teaching these students requires the understanding of differing ethnic and cultural backgrounds and a knowledge of the ways in which individuals value and approach the learning experience. Age, gender, and educational preparation also must be considered if we are to educate our entire population.

Third, developments in cognitive psychology and learning theory are beginning to unveil the differing ways in which people learn. No longer can we treat students, even those from the same ethnic and socioeconomic backgrounds, as homogeneous groups of learners with identical or similar needs. Further study of brain and mind will lead to further insights, but even today's TAs need to be prepared to work with students who have learning disabilities—students clearly bright enough to do university work but disabled in their processing of information—as well as with the majority group of learners, who bring a wide array of learning styles to classrooms.

The quest to match teaching styles and learning styles will continue. As students have become more conscious of how they learn, they now demand that TAs—and professors—demonstrate flexibility and adaptability, characteristics of very experienced teachers, in their teaching. As we conceptualize undergraduates as information processors incorporating new knowledge with prior understanding, our teaching methods must reflect that conceptualization. TAs need to learn these methods.

Fourth, demands have increased in the scholarly aspects of graduate TAs' lives. They must master their disciplines' increasingly complex knowledge and must respond to an increasing demand for predoctoral publications in many disciplines and confusing messages from mentors. "Caught in the double bind of being expected to teach well, yet being told that teaching is not important, many TAs dissociate themselves from their teaching assignments" (Wilson and Stearns, 1985, pp. 35-36). These confusing messages do little to clarify TAs' roles and responsibilities as undergraduate instructors, much less the importance of the experience as an internship for an academic career.

Fifth, in the midst of all this complexity, repeated calls for better undergraduate education are heard from national commissions, future employers, parents of undergraduates, and higher education critics. We even hear the cry from TAs themselves who wish their teaching of undergraduates had been a better experience.

Adjusting to rapid developments in knowledge, to students' diversity, to developments in the psychology of learning, and to the emphasis on the quality of undergraduate education requires much of today's TAs. The issues are even more complex because TAs are part of a large, interdependent system. Relationships that influence TAs' performance include their bonds with other TAs, with their TA supervisors, with their undergraduate students, and with their institutions. Developers of effective TA training programs must recognize all these factors and their interdependence.

Conceptualizing the Challenge

Recent educational developments require alterations in some of the assumptions we have made about how we train TAs. We need to move beyond an input-output model that focuses solely on the TA and assumes that TAs can directly apply whatever instructional skills or information we give them. Instead, we need to develop a more complete understanding of what happens to TAs as they learn to fulfill their tasks. That understanding will come from a slightly different conceptualization of TA training, one that focuses on the multiple dimensions of the TA experience and also on the interrelatedness of these dimensions.

The Dimensions. The TA experience does not occur in isolation but is affected by a variety of factors. TAs receive numerous messages and interact with many constituencies. These experiences affect how TAs see their roles and assignments. An effective TA training program must recognize the various dimensions of TAs' experiences: the needs and characteristics of the TAs themselves, as well as the relationships that TAs have with other TAs, the demands of the students they teach, the expectations of supervisors and administrators, and, sometimes, the requirements of instructional developers. In addition, TAs have departmentally specified responsibilities. All these factors have to be considered if we are to train TAs in ways that realistically address the issues they face as beginning teachers and as professors of the future.

Interrelatedness of the Dimensions. A more complete conceptualization of TA training suggests that we focus not only on the dimensions of the TA experience but also on their interrelatedness. This focus on how these factors fit together provides the real issues for TA training. For example, assume that our goal is to help TAs learn to give effective lectures. Conceptualizing this goal in terms of interrelated factors suggests that we cannot focus on lecturing skills as separate from the other dimensions that may simultaneously affect how TAs lecture; rather, we have to think about a specific TA or group of TAs lecturing to a specific group of students—who, for example, learn best through demonstration. To carry the example one step farther, we need to think about teaching a specific group of TAs to lecture to a group of students who learn best through demonstration, in a department that traditionally has not provided TAs with the kinds of equipment necessary to conduct in-class demonstrations. The training for these TAs is not so much a matter of developing their lecturing skills (which may be applicable only in specific cases) as it is a matter of developing their skills in demonstrating major concepts and using creative strategies that do not require expensive equipment.

As another example, imagine that our goal is to help TAs learn to lead effective quiz sections. In this case, the lectures and the readings cover large amounts of information. Experienced TAs have told the new TAs that, without some kind of active learning strategy, students are simply unable to retain large amounts of information. Some students prefer to have time to clarify, discuss, and question the information, while others want TAs in the quiz sections to help them determine what is most important of all the information presented. In this scenario, it may be ineffective to provide TAs with general skills in leading quiz sections; instead, TAs need ways to balance the variety of demands being placed on them by a professor's expectations, students' learning styles, and their own lack of experience. The training, then, could focus on facilitating highly task-oriented small groups, structured to provide emphasis on important concepts and to encourage and respond to students' questions in ways that help students clarify the material in their own terms. With this focus for the training, the tightly structured small groups would allow the TAs to cover much of the important information. The interaction in small groups would provide opportunities for students to discuss, ask questions, and clarify in ways that would help them retain more of the course content, and the synthesis of information would provide the opportunity for TAs to emphasize important concepts.

Although these examples could be approached in a variety of ways, they reinforce the importance of TA training that focuses on all the factors that influence what TAs actually do in their teaching. Only when we conceptualize TA training in this way can we offer TAs the kind of balance necessary to fulfill their roles successfully.

The Challenge. The challenge of the 1990s is to identify and address issues that arise when we conceptualize TA training as a process of helping TAs balance the many dimensions that affect their experience. Although this conceptualization of TA training increases the difficulty of the training task, it is too important to ignore. It provides the only realistic way to identify the teaching and career issues that TAs face and to produce a higher quality of TA training programs.

How do we begin to respond to this challenge? We need to take seriously the charge that TA training is important to the quality of undergraduate instruction and to the preparation of future professors. As part of the new conceptualization, we need to know more about the stages of TAs' development, TAs' socialization, the styles of TAs' supervisors, the diverse needs of undergraduates, and the constraining characteristics of university culture. We also need to analyze how these factors are interrelated, so that we can assist TAs, removing ambiguity in the messages they receive and reconciling inconsistencies by developing strategies that they can apply directly to their teaching. Another way to proceed is to identify the variety of people on individual campuses who can make significant contributions to TA training. Once we identify the individuals who can provide a variety of perspectives for training programs, we must seek ways for them to collaborate in meeting the specific needs of TAs. Finally, we must do the research that will allow us to identify important dimensions of the TA experience, determine how those dimensions are interrelated, prepare TAs for the issues that arise from those interrelationships, and assess the effects of the resulting training. We must examine not only the effects of one training program compared to another but also the ways specific factors interact within each program to influence effectiveness. We must also move beyond measures of TAs' and students' satisfaction with various training procedures, to include the effects of training on the development of TAs and the learning of undergraduates.

This more complex conceptualization demands meaningful discussion among all parties involved in TA training if we are to help TAs meet the challenge of the 1990s. That discussion should allow us to see the complexity and subtleties of the TA experience and develop specific ways to enable TAs to be effective in their instructional roles. This time we must act—and produce results—if we hope to provide TA training that enhances both the quality of undergraduate education and the possibility that outstanding graduate TAs will become the professors of tomorrow.

References

Andrews, J.D.W. (ed.). *Strengthening the Teaching Assistant Faculty.* New Directions for Teaching and Learning, no. 22. San Francisco: Jossey-Bass, 1985.

Green, M. F. (ed.). *Minorities on Campus: A Handbook for Enhancing Diversity.* Washington, D.C.: American Council on Education, 1988.

Laing, G. J. "The Newer Educational Program and the Training of Teachers." In W. S. Gray (ed.), *The Training of College Teachers, Including Their Preliminary Preparation and In-Service Improvement.* Chicago: The University of Chicago Press, 1930.

Nyquist, J. D., and Wulff, D. H. "The Training of Graduate Teaching Assistants at the University of Washington." In N. Van Note Chism (ed.), *Employment and Education of Teaching Assistants: Readings from a National Conference.* Columbus: Center for Teaching Excellence, Ohio State University, 1987.

Wilson, T., and Stearns, J. "Improving the Working Relationship Between Professor and TA." In J.D.W. Andrews (ed.), *Strengthening the Teaching Assistant Faculty.* New Directions for Teaching and Learning, no. 22. San Francisco: Jossey-Bass, 1985.

Wise, W. M. "Who Teaches the Teachers?" In C.B.T. Lee (ed.), *Improving College Teaching.* Washington, D.C.: American Council on Education, 1967.

Jody D. Nyquist is a lecturer in the Department of Speech Communication and is director for instructional development at the Center for Instructional Development and Research, University of Washington.

Robert D. Abbott is professor of educational psychology and director for program research at the Center for Instructional Development and Research, University of Washington.

Donald H. Wulff is assistant director of the Center for Instructional Development and Research, University of Washington.

Socialization of TAs occurs through a process of communication as newcomers learn what it means to be teachers as well as graduate students.

Socialization of Teaching Assistants

Ann Q. Staton, Ann L. Darling

The role of the teaching assistant (TA) in American colleges and universities is a complex and multifaceted one. At first glance, two major components of the role emerge: a TA is a graduate student and at the same time a teacher. These two components are distinct, perhaps even disparate, and yet TAs are expected to integrate them and enact each one with skill and expertise. The nature of the two components is such that success in one role does not necessarily imply success in the other; indeed, success in one can even detract from success in the other.

Being simultaneously a student and a teacher can be difficult. As Boehrer and Sarkisian (1985) point out, "The principal irony of the TA's situation is that of occupying the teaching role because of having been a successful student" (p. 16). They go on to say, "The essence of teaching is to facilitate rather than display learning" (p. 16). The time demands of being either an effective teacher or an outstanding student are stringent and often overwhelming, and TAs must maintain a constant balance between the two tasks. As one TA commented, this balance is not easy to accomplish: "When I set my own work as a priority over grading papers, my students don't understand, and when I sacrifice classwork for teaching, my professors are disappointed."

In addition to being complex because of its dual components, the TA role is unique in that it is transitional. For those who plan careers as college or university faculty members, the TA role can be considered as an internship or training period. The skills, behavior, and attitudes developed while one is a TA are important determinants of one's future faculty role. In contrast, for those who do not seek academic careers, the TA role can be considered merely a means of employment and financial support while students are completing graduate degrees. Whatever the case, there is no permanence in the TA role; no one ever had a career as a TA. By its very nature and definition, then, it is a transitory role.

This chapter focuses on what occurs during that transition period by examining the socialization of TAs. First, we address the nature of TA socialization and its various dimensions. Second, we discuss how the process of socialization occurs through communication. Third, we present implications for the development of TA training programs.

Dimensions of Socialization

Socialization is defined as "the process by which people selectively acquire the values and attitudes, the interests, skills and knowledge—in short the culture—current in groups to which they are, or seek to become, a member" (Merton, Reader, and Kendall, 1957, p. 287). Although views of the process vary, much recent research has examined socialization from a dialectical perspective (Zeichner, 1980). According to this view, newcomers to a role or to an organization engage actively with others in the environment—to construct appropriate roles for themselves, to carve out suitable niches, and to meet their individual needs (Staton-Spicer and Darling, 1986, 1987). When this perspective is applied to the socialization of TAs, it becomes apparent that both role and cultural socialization occur.

Role Socialization. Role socialization involves learning the functions, expectations, and requirements of a new role and developing one's own way of performing the role (Sarbin and Allen, 1968). TAs entering a graduate program socialize to both components of their role: graduate student and teacher. In addition, because the TA role is a transitory one that often provides passage into the academy, the experience of being a TA becomes the means of socialization to the professoriate.

Socialization to the role of graduate student involves socialization to academic life (as a student working on an advanced degree) and to a particular discipline and field of study. Although all persons entering a graduate program have spent many years as students, the role of student has not remained constant. Indeed, the role changes considerably over the student's career, from elementary school to graduate school (Staton, in press). The TA must assume the role of advanced learner. The tasks that absorb the graduate student include a variety of learning activities:

attending classes, completing course assignments, working with faculty on research projects, passing comprehensive or qualifying examinations, writing theses or dissertations, and so forth.

In addition, new graduate students select particular fields of specialty within their disciplines and undergo a process of socialization to their disciplines. Unlike most undergraduate majors, who generally leave with the B.A. or B.S. degree and a broad understanding of their fields as a whole, graduate students actively seek a deeper understanding of their chosen areas of study and often begin to reshape their identities in ways that define themselves as members of their respective academic disciplines. This is particularly true at the Ph.D. level, where the goal of contributing knowledge to the discipline involves an even more complex understanding and level of commitment.

For graduate students, socialization to the teaching role may be more unfamiliar. After having been students for many years, TAs are suddenly thrust into the new role of teacher. During socialization, novices take on the identity of teacher (they see themselves as teachers) and perform the functions of a teacher (engage in specific kinds of behavior). The tasks that absorb the TA who is functioning as a teacher include planning classes, generating assignments, meeting with students, leading discussions or quiz sections, grading papers, and so forth. TAs begin to think, feel, and act the way teachers do, constructing "teacher" roles that are distinct and uniquely their own.

Finally, the TA role may also socialize students to the role of professor or faculty member. The TA experience is frequently the only and best preparation for becoming a professor. TAs who must balance the heavy demands of teaching and their own work begin to develop a sense of the role of a faculty member who must teach and conduct research.

Cultural Socialization. The second dimension is cultural socialization. The actual tasks of the graduate student and teaching roles may be similar across departments and universities, but social practices, collective understandings, attitudes, and values take on a cultural flavor unique to specific departments. New TAs, even those who have been TAs at other institutions, are outsiders who need "a sense of the feel, the smell, the personality of a workplace, a way of working, or a kind of work" (Louis, 1985, p. 27). The new TAs must learn the norms of a particular department on a particular university campus. Thus, socialization to the culture of a department is still another dimension of the process.

How Socialization Occurs

Socialization to the TA role occurs through a process of communication—that is, new TAs learn how to understand and work with their new colleagues, enact the role of advanced student, fulfill the responsibilities of a teacher, and develop values and beliefs about the academic profession while observing, sharing, and responding to messages in the new environment. Through the process of communication, TAs develop a social support system, obtain information, adjust to rules and policies, and generate new ideas about teaching and research.

Developing a Social Support System. New friendships are a vital component of the TA socialization experience. In fact, having a group of people with whom one can share concerns, fears, triumphs, and challenges during graduate school can make a considerable difference in later success as a faculty member (Pavalko and Holley, 1974). Such groups help new TAs survive the stress of balancing both dimensions of the TA role by providing emotional reassurance and practical assistance.

Darling (1988), drawing from qualitative case-study data from five new TAs, reported that TAs devote as much as 88 percent of their interactions to building and maintaining personal relationships with new TA colleagues. So important were such relationships that when two individuals felt isolated from the group of new TAs, each went out of her way to spend more time in the department and schedule social activities with colleagues. Somewhat surprisingly, new TAs appear to socialize themselves, rather than to be socialized by experienced members of the department. The social support system creates a context in which new TAs share interpretations of the department and its people, anxieties about teaching, and responses to graduate coursework. In effect, new TAs say to each other, "This is what I see going on here and how I feel about it. How does this resonate with your impressions?" In two separate investigations, Darling (1986, 1987) found that new TAs spend most of their communication time interacting with peers. These interactions serve primarily to create a sense of community or build a system of support. In the words of one new TA, "We support each other in this; we help each other in any way that we can. That is what graduate school is all about."

Obtaining Information. One of the biggest challenges of socialization is to acquire sufficient information (Jablin, 1987). New TAs need information about what is expected of them as teachers and graduate students, about resources, about the new people and the new setting, and about how their behavior is perceived by others in the department. A number of different sources can provide information, some of which can be presented directly and explicitly by the department during orientation programs (Darling and Staton-Spicer, 1986). Ultimately, however, it is impossible for the department, or any other socializing agency alone, to provide enough information in sufficient detail for the individual to navigate the socialization experience successfully (Darling and Staton, in press; Rosen and Bates, 1968). Therefore, it is important that new TAs acquire appropriate communication strategies of their own to gain information.

Berger (1986) articulates three types of information-seeking strategies—passive, active, and interactive—that individuals use during the developing stages of an interpersonal relationship, and Darling (1986) examined how these strategies were used by new TAs during the initial phase of socialization. She found that individuals used passive strategies (for example, observing others and listening to others' conversations) to get information about how to manage interactions with the faculty and about how to present themselves as professional scholars. Boehrer and Sarkisian (1985) also discovered that new TAs used watching and eavesdropping to get information about the value that was placed on the TA role by individuals of higher status.

TAs in Darling's (1986) study also asked third parties (an active strategy) and consulted the most direct source of information (an interactive strategy). When TAs needed information that was highly salient, risky, and unobtainable through observation, they typically consulted a reliable third party (for example, they asked an experienced TA how a particular professor would be likely to respond to a challenge). Only when the information concerned something of low risk (for example, how to approach a particular topic in class, or whether there would be changes in the schedule) were new TAs likely to consult professors directly.

Adapting to Rules and Procedures. New TAs need to obtain information by using communication strategies, and through communication they also make sense of unfamiliar policies and procedures. New TAs are sometimes dismayed to discover that they have inadvertently broken rules or violated policies. For example, one individual in Darling's (1986) study allowed undergraduates to use her notes to study for an exam, and she was caught completely by surprise when the professor announced in lecture that none of his TAs would commit such a violation of policy. She became distraught by what she had done, checked with a number of new TAs to determine whether they had ever shown undergraduates their notes, asked several experienced TAs what she should do to correct the matter, and finally apologized to the professor and the undergraduates for the misunderstanding.

Rules and procedures, like information, are not always clearly and coherently presented. It is nearly impossible for socialization agents to present completely all the rules and policies that guide conduct in a role and a department. Some rules may not even be widely known, or they may be so taken for granted that they cannot be articulated. Thus, through communication new TAs come to understand and engage in appropriate rule-governed behavior.

TAs communicate in ways that facilitate their participation in the rule-governed dimension of role enactment and organizational membership. For example, according to Darling's (1987) work, new TAs ask for advice, feedback, and permission. In so doing, they invite others to participate in controlling or regulating their behavior. New TAs also engage in regulation of others. As teachers, they describe and maintain policies about classroom instruction and departmental functions. As graduate students, they exert control collectively (for example, by challenging a professor's decision about a final exam date). Such expressions of control contribute to the development of a role identity, and help new TAs feel like teachers. New TAs also use communication behavior to reject control. Such behavior as justifying, avoiding, and refusing may be employed to avert being controlled in unacceptable ways.

Generating New Ideas. Not all the problems facing new TAs can be resolved through acquiring information or adapting. TAs must confront unique problems surrounded by special circumstances. In some instances, the problem is old (for example, how to teach grammar in a stimulating and relevant way), and yet no adequate solution is known to the TAs.

Brainstorming, sharing ideas, and exchanging perspectives are all communication strategies that individuals employ to generate solutions to these perplexing problems. One group of TAs in Darling's (1988) study reported that brainstorming sessions occurred whenever anyone raised a new problem for the others, either about teaching or about research. Together, the new TAs identified solutions which individuals could select and modify to meet their own needs. Another group of TAs used brainstorming and idea sharing to reduce the amount of time they had to spend on their teaching (Darling, 1986). The effect of these brainstorming sessions went beyond immediate problems. TAs reported that the chance to meet and talk about ideas with their peers enabled them to develop a larger and more precise picture of the various ways in which people teach and conduct academic research. Further, such discussions enabled TAs to broaden their own repertoires of appropriate strategies for teaching and conducting research. Finally, TAs reported feeling more like members of the academy simply because they had participated in the generating and analyzing of ideas (Darling, 1988).

Implications for TA Training

Communication during TA socialization serves four distinct functions: to help the TA to develop a social support system, obtain information, adjust to rules and policies, and generate new ideas about teaching and research. Those involved in the preparation of TAs may want to consider designing training programs that will be sensitive to each of these four functions. Both the orientation program that greets new TAs and the sessions that occur throughout the first term or first year should reflect an understanding of these four types of needs. For instance, it takes time for friendships to develop and for support networks to form. Similarly, newcomers cannot assimilate large bodies of critical information in a brief period. Many cultural norms and assumptions are not even consciously articulated by group members but must be learned over time by newcomers as they interact with others. TAs must also interact with undergraduates before their need to share information about teaching is acute. An awareness of the socialization process experienced by TAs facilitates decisions about the types of training that would be most optimal.

Our research suggests that such ideas as encouraging senior TAs to provide social events for new TAs, explicitly teaching new TAs how to ask questions to gain information, and providing opportunities for them to brainstorm with one another about teaching and research could become important aspects of TA training programs. In addition, program designers may want to consider what our research suggests about the role of experienced TAs. Since they function as primary informants for new TAs, their information about changes in departmental and graduate school policies must be accurate and up to date. Since new TAs may be reluctant to ask professors questions, except in low-risk cases, experienced TAs can be critical sources of information about expectations, policies, procedures, and new ideas for teaching. This finding suggests that experienced TAs should be made aware of their important role and given tools to help in mentoring new TAs. This reliance on peers also suggests that the veteran TA should be involved actively in the actual training programs for new TAs, not only as a presenter but also as an informal information source about life as a TA in the department.

Conclusion

Becoming a TA is a complex process. It involves becoming familiar with the ways and meanings of being both a student and a teacher in a particular department. It also involves becoming knowledgeable in a specific discipline. This process is one with both short- and long-term consequences. In the most immediate sense, socialization affects attitudes about and behavior in the TA role. In a more enduring sense, however, the process of becoming a TA influences the thoughts and feelings one has about the academy, as well as the types of activities one pursues as a professor.

References

Berger, C. R. "Communication Under Uncertainty." In M. E. Roloff and G. R. Miller (eds.), *Further Explorations in Interpersonal Communication*. Newbury Park, Calif.: Sage, 1986.

Boehrer, J., and Sarkisian, E. "The Teaching Assistant's Point of View." In J.D.W. Andrews (ed.), *Strengthening the Teaching Assistant Faculty*. New Directions for Teaching and Learning, no. 22. San Francisco: Jossey-Bass, 1985.

Darling, A. L. "On Becoming a Graduate Student: An Examination of Communication in the Socialization Process." Paper presented at the annual meeting of the Speech Communication Association, Chicago, 1986.

Darling, A. L. "Communication in Graduate Teaching Assistant Socialization: Encounters and Strategies." Paper presented at the annual meeting of the Speech Communication Association, Boston, November 1987.

Darling, A. L. "Graduate Student Socialization: Categories of Encounters." Paper presented at the annual meeting of the International Communication Association, New Orleans, May 1988.

Darling, A. L., and Staton, A. Q. "Socialization of Graduate Teaching Assistants: A Case Study in an American University." *International Journal of Qualitative Studies in Education*, in press.

Darling, A. L., and Staton-Spicer, A. Q. "Communication in the Socialization of Graduate TAs: An Ethnographic Study." Paper presented at the annual meeting of the American Education Research Association Convention, San Francisco, April 1986.

Jablin, F. M. "Organizational Entry, Assimilation, and Exit." In F. M. Jablin, L. L. Putnam, K. H. Roberts, and L. W. Porter (eds.), *Handbook of Organizational Communication*. Newbury Park, Calif.: Sage, 1987.

Louis, M. R. "Perspectives on Organization Culture." In P. J. Frost, L. F. Moore, M. R. Louis, C. C. Lundberg, and J. Martin (eds.), *Organizational Culture*. Newbury Park, Calif.: Sage, 1985.

Merton, R., Reader, G., and Kendall, P. *The Student Physician*. Cambridge, Mass.: Harvard University Press, 1957.

Pavalko, R. M., and Holley, J. W. "Determinants of Professional Self-Concept Among Graduate Students." *Social Science Quarterly*, 1974, 55, 462-477.

Rosen, B. C., and Bates, A. P. "The Structure of Socialization in Graduate School." *Sociological Inquiry*, 1968, 37, 71-84.

Sarbin, T. R., and Allen, V. L. "Role Theory." In G. Lindzey and E. Aronson (eds.), *The Handbook of Social Psychology*. Reading, Mass.: Addison-Wesley, 1968.

Staton, A. Q. *Communication and Student Socialization*. Norwood, N.J.: Ablex, in press.

Staton-Spicer, A. Q., and Darling, A. L. "Communication in the Socialization of Preservice Teachers." *Communication Education*, 1986, 35, 215-230.

Staton-Spicer, A. Q., and Darling, A. L. "A Communication Perspective on Teacher Socialization." *Journal of Thought*, 1987, 22, 12-19.

Zeichner, K. M. "Key Processes in the Socialization of Student Teachers: Limitations and Consequences of Oversocialized Conceptions of Teacher Socialization." Paper presented at the annual meeting of the American Educational Research Association, Boston, April 1980.

Ann Q. Staton is associate professor and chair of the Department of Speech Communication, University of Washington.

Ann L. Darling is assistant professor in the Department of Speech Communication, University of Illinois-Urbana.

Faculty members in the future need to develop special sensitivities and alternative teaching strategies to be responsive to an increasingly diverse student body.

Teaching in a Diverse Environment: Knowledge and Skills Needed by TAs

Nancy Van Note Chism, Jamie Cano, Anne S. Pruitt

Over the past thirty years, colleges and universities have become accessible to many types of students who previously did not attend in great numbers. Among these are ethnic minorities, returning adults, and students with disabilities. In addition, the special characteristics of other populations, such as women and gay and lesbian students, have been recognized more widely. Although increases in participation rates have not been steady, particularly for minority students, demographic projections, as well as new pressures on colleges and universities to renew their efforts to recruit and retain a diverse population, indicate that the student population of the future will be a very diverse one (Green, 1988).

Although changes in student population have been taking place, very few changes have occurred in the way in which universities approach teaching and learning. Students from nontraditional groups have simply been expected to adjust to the prevailing environment and culture of the classroom. The curriculum is heavily based on the Western intellectual tradition, and expectations for students are based on years of experience with young white males from college-preparatory programs. Changes, such as the emergence of black studies and women's studies and a variety of support services for ethnic minorities, older students, and students with disabilities, have usually been introduced as alternative opportunities for students. Most universities have not yet found ways to integrate appreciation and respect for students' diversity into regular curriculum offerings, instructional strategies, and expectations or to benefit from the insights, perspectives, and cultural knowledge that these new student populations possess.

A crucial figure in efforts to make the university more responsive to students' diversity will be the professor of the future. Many studies have documented the pivotal role that the professor plays in students' success (Astin, 1975; Sedlacek, 1983). If universities are to benefit from the perspectives that nontraditional students bring, and if they want to provide successful learning experiences for these students, they must prepare the instructors who will interact daily with students. Consequently, teaching assistants (TAs), both in their present roles as primary support staff in undergraduate instruction and in their future roles as faculty members, must prepare to teach in ways that will benefit their students as well as their universities.

This chapter provides an overview of what TAs and future professors must know to teach nontraditional students. It discusses significant characteristics of each group, suggests ways for faculty members to help students from these groups achieve success, and recommends ways in which those intending to be professors can prepare to teach effectively in a diverse environment.

Characteristics of Nontraditional Students

Ethnic Minorities. Students from the main ethnic minority groups in this country—black Americans, Hispanic Americans, Asian Americans, and native Americans—often find matriculation at predominantly white campuses disconcerting. Like white students, they are suddenly expected to be quite independent in an unfamiliar environment, and they may be experiencing the first prolonged stay away from home. In addition to these common adjustment problems, however, they may experience sharp cultural differences and extra pressures that make adjustment all the harder. Pemberton (1988) describes these problems and the impact they have on minority students. Depending on their previous life situations, the students may experience financial stress, absence of friends from the usual peer group, lack of familiar cultural opportunities, unfamiliar food and customs, and confusion about bureaucratic procedures. Nontraditional students may also be subjected to racism, sexism, and the curiosity or hostility of students, staff, and instructors. If they are the first in their families to go to college or are conscious of extreme financial hardship that their education is causing their families, they may put enormous pressure on themselves. If they come from poor educational backgrounds, they may fear being inadequately prepared for college work.

Students from ethnic minority groups respond to these pressures in a variety of ways. Some adapt or develop an inner strength that enables them to succeed; others become alienated and adopt attitudes that appear to be defensive, hostile, or defeatist; still others may become increasingly anxious, lonely, and fearful and may withdraw. Their expectations of themselves may range across extremes, from an inordinate fear of failure to an unrealistically high self-perception.

Within and across ethnic groups, there are great differences in how students respond to the college environment. An upper-middle-class Hispanic student may experience no unusual difficulties, but a student coming directly from a lower-class family may have major cultural disorientation. An Asian American student from a family that emphasizes extreme diligence and quiet, reserved behavior will respond differently from an Asian American student whose family encourages assertiveness and is more relaxed about academic achievement. Some black American students will struggle with differences in way of speaking, sense of time, or learning styles, while others will have characteristics that already resemble those of the dominant culture. Native Americans may be more contemplative and nature-oriented that other students, or they may be no different with respect to these traits, since much depends on the extent to which a given student has experienced and incorporated the characteristics of the majority culture.

Returning Adults. Like ethnic minority students, returning adults display marked differences among themselves. Some may be homemakers who interrupted their studies to raise children; others may be retired business executives who want to pursue work in fields that always interested them. They may have excellent prior academic backgrounds, or they may have fulfilled minimum requirements for admission. These students may be financially stressed, or they may be very secure. They may be very healthy, or they may be experiencing such age-related problems as diminished hearing or eyesight. They may come with or without the academic skills that most faculty members expect.

Most older adults in higher education experience self-consciousness and anxiety about their age and performance. They may feel more obligation to please the instructor than younger students do. They may be too modest about their own abilities and experiences. They may seek more reassurance from instructors, and they may need to verbalize more than younger students do. On the other hand, older students may be more impatient with activities that they feel are not useful in their learning, and they may argue with instructors who present information or ideas that are not consistent with their experiences. Although adjustment for older students sometimes progresses very smoothly, it is often extremely difficult.

Students with Disabilities. Another group characterized by its internal diversity is the group of students with disabilities. Whether the disabilities are physical or related to learning, these students display a variety of differences that directly affect instruction. Students with learning disabilities have average or above-average intelligence but experience differences in the processes involved in listening, thinking, speaking, reading, or computation (Hammill, Leigh, McNutt, and Larsen, 1981). Students with such conditions as perceptual handicaps, brain injury, minimal brain dysfunction, dyslexia, and developmental aphasia fall into this category. Students with physical handicaps have learning problems that are the result of visual, hearing, or motor disorders.

Like students from other nontraditional populations, students with disabilities are self-conscious and anxious about their ability to perform. Especially when there is an undiagnosed learning disability, a student may experience continual frustration. It is often very difficult for students with disabilities to identify their problems and express their special needs to faculty members. They may not be sure of what help they need, or they may feel that they will be resented for asking for special arrangements. Some of these students have few difficulties functioning in the university environment, but many experience severe hardship.

Women Students. Although women have been part of the college scene for many years, classroom practices that have arisen through a tradition of male-dominated instructional settings still detract from learning opportunities for women. These practices are well documented in Hall and Sandler (1982). Like the other groups, women who attend college come from diverse backgrounds, have different kinds of academic preparation and abilities, and have different ways of perceiving and responding to social norms. Some women lack confidence in their abilities, are eager to please, put other priorities before formal studies, and think about the world and express themselves in experientially based ways. Other women are just the opposite, and many more are somewhere in between. When differences arise between the university's traditional practices and women's performance or expectations, women, sensing that their contributions are devalued, may feel angry or inadequate. Sexism can be subtle, and women may blame themselves for problems and may try to adapt, or they may withdraw. Thus, new insights and contributions that women could bring to scholarship are often curtailed.

Gay and Lesbian Students. Gay and lesbian students are often called the "invisible minority" (Crumpbacker and Vander Haegen, 1984) because they are not easily identifiable. Although many people think that gay and lesbian students can be identified by their dress or mannerisms, such assumptions rest on stereotypic descriptions, which are often as erroneous as the stereotypes of other groups. Current statistics estimate that one in every ten students is gay or lesbian and that sexual preference is not unchanging or one-dimensional over the course of a lifetime. Therefore, it is likely that gay and lesbian students are more numerous in college classrooms than most instructors realize, and that students may change their sexual preference and self-identifications over the course of their college career and lifetimes. As with other special populations, gay and lesbian students are diverse in their learning styles, their backgrounds, their academic preparation and abilities, and their personalities. One shared concern among many gay and lesbian students is anxiety about self-disclosure. In an environment in which heterosexuality is assumed and hostility toward other sexual preferences prevails, they are likely to fear the social disapproval or even violence that their disclosure may prompt. Often, gay or lesbian students may be struggling with their identity, dealing with feelings of inadequacy, shame, and anger resulting from past experiences with social intolerance. The "invisible" status of this population, the silent suffering that many students endure, and the homophobia that pervades our society make the problems of gay and lesbian students particularly difficult.

Few meaningful commonalities can be applied to students from diverse populations. Within and across groups, differences exist in individual learning preferences, educational background and aspirations, values, cultural experiences, and aptitudes. To the extent that students from nontraditional groups have participated in and adapted to mainstream culture in educational settings, they resemble the traditional population. Those who have not participated or who have not adapted may face severe adjustments and, perhaps, defeat by the forces that work against their success.

In the face of such diversity both within and across groups, there is no one set of teaching strategies that will advance the cause of nontraditional students' success; rather, instructors can take a basic student-centered stance to enhance the success of these students. Such a stance places value on treating students as individuals and encouraging their participation in learning. This stance goes beyond laying out the feast of knowledge and being indifferent about whether all partake; it accepts responsibility for welcoming students and for creating conditions for their success as inherent parts of an instructor's role. For TAs and future faculty members, the task is to plan learning experiences that help all students feel that their world views are accepted and valued, know that they form an essential part of the class, perceive themselves to be good students, and dare to try new tasks with expectations of success.

Ways for Instructors to Help

The traditional approach to college teaching has centered on subject matter; yet, as Banks (1988) points out, instructors need to think first in terms of teaching students, not subjects. To be effective with a diverse student population, instructors particularly need to care not only about how they organize and present content but also about how successful they are in reaching students. They need to know their students, be continually alert to students' nonverbal behavior in class, make provisions for frequent feedback, and involve students as active participants.

Treating Students as Individuals. The possibility that stereotypes will influence an instructor's expectations is particularly strong for nontraditional groups. Black students, for example, recount that instructors often assume that they are athletes, are surprised when they hand in well-written reports (black students who write well are frequently suspected of plagiarism), and expect them to have come from inferior high schools. Asian Americans report that instructors often imply that they will be mathematically inclined and more studious and self-motivated than others. These descriptions are accurate for some students, but not for all or even most. To loosen the hold of stereotypes, instructors must struggle to broaden their unconscious assumptions by getting to know individual students.

There are many things that instructors can do to get to know their students. Asking students to talk about themselves, either in writing or orally, at the beginning of the term can be invaluable in building group cohesion, as well as in alerting the instructor to the special characteristics of each student. Administering a pretest or taking a writing sample early in the term can provide a data-based picture of entry levels. Arriving early for class and engaging students in conversation outside class can further increase the kind of particular knowledge that keeps stereotypes from dominating.

Instructors need to be especially sensitive in their attempts to get to know students from nontraditional groups. These students often will not want to be singled out for special consideration, and so care must be taken to get to know students from traditional groups as well. Since students who are uncomfortable in the university environment may suspect ulterior motives on the part of instructors, it is important to convey goodwill and not to force disclosure beyond what students volunteer. Any invitation to meet outside the classroom should also be made in nonthreatening and cordial ways.

Another strategy for highlighting the unique characteristics of the students in a class is to ask students to relate the course content to their own experiences. Providing such opportunities for discussion allows students to present information on their unique backgrounds and characteristics. For example, a woman could illustrate how a mechanical principle that has just been described applies to her previous experience as an auto mechanic. By so doing, she would dispel some stereotypes that the instructor and her classmates might have held.

Preventing Discrimination in the Classroom. Despite the instructor's efforts to recognize the individuality of students, the discrimination that is so prevalent in our society may also manifest itself in the classroom. Racial slurs, and jokes about women, gays and lesbians, minority groups, older people, and people with disabilities, must be dealt with directly, rather than avoided. More subtle are such language-embedded problems as "Let's hear from the gals on this" and "They were crippled in their efforts to discover the cause" and "I'm in a really black mood today"—phrases that are not meant to disparage groups of people, but they can have that effect. Remarks about a woman's appearance, even when the remark is a compliment, are perceived by many women as reinforcing the notion of women as sexual objects.

Additional problems occur with the preferences of groups for self-identifying labels, which are often debated within a group itself. *Hispanic,* for example, is the preferred designation of some people, but many people of Mexican American or Puerto Rican origin prefer such terms as *Chicano* or *Latino,* which refer to their more immediate origins, rather than to Spain. Some students with disabilities may prefer the term *differently abled* to *disabled* or *handicapped.* Although instructors should certainly avoid using obviously offensive terms, it may be necessary to check the preferences of students regarding terms on which there is currently discussion, such as *African American* versus *black.*

When overtly discriminatory language is used in the classroom, it may seem easier to pass over the issue quickly and hope that no offense was taken, but this response perpetuates the problem. A brief, firm comment, pointing out that sexist jokes will not be permitted or that the preferred term is *Asian American,* rather than *Oriental,* can establish nondiscriminatory norms in a class and alert students to ways in which they unintentionally offend others. Similarly, instructors can ask students to alert them when they themselves say things that are offensive. Nonverbal communication can also be perceived as discriminatory. Touching women, or using gestures or winks, may be perceived as sexual harassment, and failing to make eye contact with some students causes them to feel excluded.

Encouraging Full Participation. Student-centered teaching requires an interactive element. If lecturing is the primary strategy, frequent pauses to check for comprehension, allow for questions, and make occasions for students to relate the topic to their own experience are important. When using discussions, role playing, laboratory or project work, and group work, instructors should ensure that students from nontraditional groups participate fully.

Participation in classroom discussion is particularly important, but there are some pitfalls. Students from nontraditional groups may feel that they are ignored or that they are being forced to participate, and so it is important to be sensitive. A common mistake of instructors is to call on minority students to present "the minority point of view." A seemingly innocent request by an instructor—"Tell us, Marcie, how blacks evaluate the impact of the civil rights movement"—puts the student in the position of having to speak for an entire group whose members probably have different perspectives. Instructors should be careful to let students choose to participate voluntarily and should encourage involvement by making eye contact, posing open questions, and welcoming participation when it does occur. If students from nontraditional groups are especially reticent, an encouraging talk outside class may help. In the end, however, the desire to be quiet should be respected.

The instructor should also exercise caution when laboratory or project teams and leaders are chosen. If groups tend to segregate themselves or exclude certain students, the instructor can help provide more opportunities for involvement by assigning groups, counting off, or drawing names, rather than by allowing students to self-select. As the groups work, the instructor should mingle and try to correct any instances of exclusion or devaluation that occur. The instructor can further encourage students to interact by creating study groups or task groups, which can present occasions for students to get to know one another outside the class. Students from nontraditional groups may often need extra encouragement to participate and to take on leadership roles.

Course Design Issues. Whenever possible, students should be exposed to or made aware of the accomplishments of minority and nontraditional scholars in a discipline. When instructors are not knowledgeable about this aspect of their subject areas, they should certainly make efforts to augment their learning. They may also ask students (without singling out any particular student) who have particular interests in certain areas to share their knowledge about such topics as women in the era being discussed, minority authors of the period, or minority inventors or thinkers who influenced the development of a theory or practice. Assigning special papers or projects to all students on the contributions of various groups can provide occasions for enriching knowledge.

In addition to being more inclusive in course design choices, instructors and students alike can benefit from reexamining the assumptions on which a discipline is based. For example, much of social theory, literature, and psychology is based on the assumption of heterosexuality. Gay and lesbian students relate to a broader notion of human relationships and may feel alienated when their perspective is ignored. Minority students and women may bring a different perspective to the notion of progress and the concept of time and interpersonal relationships than is normally assumed across the disciplines. Asking students to contribute in class or through out-of-class assignments on nontraditional ways of viewing the field can help both instructors and students work toward a richer conceptualization of a discipline.

A third course design consideration is free discussion of ideas. In many disciplines, it is important to openly raise issues of race, gender, age, or ability. Discussions of deviance, the social security system, or cognitive styles would be incomplete if they did not deal with these issues. The discussion should be carefully prepared, so that instructors can explore their own assumptions in advance and anticipate difficulties. Sensitivity and an open, straightforward approach during the discussion are especially important. When unfortunate situations arise spontaneously, instructors should deal with them as fully and tactfully as possible, rather than ignore them.

Using Various Teaching Methods

In past decade, considerable interest has been focused on students' learning modalities and cognitive styles. Researchers have pointed out that students have distinct preferences for the ways in which they receive information (by listening, seeing, manipulating, experiencing) and for the ways in which they process information (holistically or analytically, concretely or abstractly, and so forth). Studies have concluded that teachers need to be sensitive to the ways in which their students learn and to teach in ways that will enable students to succeed in using their preferences. Of course, instructors should also work to extend students' learning styles.

There is some discussion concerning whether certain groups of nontraditional students have characteristic learning styles. Anderson (1988) and Hilliard (1989) discuss this question with respect to minority students; Belenky and others (1987) discuss it with respect to women. The consensus seems to be that some general statements can be made, but careful attention must be given to individual differences. Once again, there is the risk of stereotyping. It is generally concluded that black, native American, Hispanic American, and women students respond better to teaching methods that emphasize group cooperation, holistic thinking, a concrete orientation, a valuing of personal knowledge, the oral tradition, and reliance on imagery and expressiveness, to provide an affective component to learning. This learning style is very different from that possessed by most college instructors, many Asian American students (Kuroiwa, 1975), and traditional students who fall at the opposite end of the continuum, with learning styles that are characterized by an independent, abstract, impersonal, written, technical orientation.

Instructors can never respond fully to each unique learning style, since they are working in group settings, but they can try to accommodate different learning styles by working harder to respect other perspectives and by providing options for participation. For example, they can let students choose from a list of term assignments: a paper, an oral report, a dramatization, an art product. They can provide opportunities for both individual and group work. In class presentations, they can vary the ways for providing instruction, relying less on lecture and more on such strategies as collaborative learning groups, simulations, case studies, and the like. They should supplement lectures and print materials with discussion, audiovisual aids, and hands-on experience whenever possible. In assessing class participation and written work, they should be open-minded about the value of personal experiences and a holistic style, rather than simply dismissing work that has these characteristics as "nonscholarly." Marienau and Chickering (1982) point out that the emphasis on personal experience is particularly important for returning adults.

In the case of students with disabilities, instructors may need to be attentive to special needs. Hearing-impaired students may need to see the instructor's lips. Dyslexic students may need extra time to complete examinations. Motor-impaired students who rely on special equipment for writing may need to tape lectures and take tests at different sites. Older students with physical impairments may need similar consideration. Instructors should maintain close contact with the office on campus that serves these students, to ensure that their needs are understood and met.

Providing Feedback and Reinforcement. An essential component of students' successful learning is prompt, honest, and frequent feedback. Such feedback is particularly important for nontraditional students, who may be anxious about their performance in a strange environment, may suspect racism or sexism, or may hold unrealistic expectations for themselves. These students need to know early in the term what the instructor's standards are and how well they are meeting those standards. Instructors may be reluctant to talk honestly with nontraditional students for fear of conflict or the appearance of discrimination or sympathy with the efforts that students have made. Tact and empathy are important, but it is far more helpful to be as straightforward as possible in providing feedback. The timing of feedback is also particularly important. Positive reinforcement is needed early, to encourage students. Messages about inadequate performance should also come early, so that students will be alerted to the possibility of failure in time to make adjustments or seek additional help. Instructors can also help nontraditional students set realistic goals and assess their overall direction and progress. Instructors may want to provide some self-evaluation activities, so that students can continually monitor their own progress.

Outside the classroom, instructors can be supportive and the encouragement of good performance can be extended. The instructor can nominate students from nontraditional groups for awards, offer to write letters of recommendation, and help students choose challenging programs in which they can succeed. Inviting successful students to lecture in a class, or pointing out their accomplishments to other students, can provide much-needed role modeling and reinforce students' pride.

In many ways, instructors can make extra efforts to teach students from nontraditional groups. Most of the strategies make sense for good teaching in general, but modifications and special considerations are important. To prepare well for teaching a diverse population, TAs should keep several things in mind before their first teaching assignments. These points are discussed in the following section.

Preparing to Teach a Diverse Group

The prevailing beliefs that teachers are born and not made and that there is nothing to learn about teaching have deemphasized the importance of teacher preparation in higher education. Many TAs and new faculty members come to their teaching responsibilities without significant teaching knowledge and without established teaching skills. At many campuses, problems caused by these conditions are gradually being addressed through new programs and services for TAs and faculty members. In addition to possessing sound general knowledge and good teaching skills, TAs and future faculty members will need to take some special steps to prepare for effectively teaching a diverse student population.

Understanding Nontraditional Learning Styles. Assuming that all members of a given group will exhibit the same learning style is a form of stereotyping, nevertheless future faculty members should be aware of the characteristics commonly associated with particular groups. Such knowledge, along with knowledge about effective teaching strategies for students with particular preferences and about expanding the range of such preferences, will enable faculty members to consider each case individually but recognize some common patterns when they occur.

Learning About the History and Culture of Nontraditional Groups. Despite their scholarship in their disciplines, TAs are often strangely unaware of the world views, literatures, customs, music, and values of their fellow Americans. Many future faculty members have not enjoyed a diversity of friendships. Exploration of these areas can lead TAs to be more understanding of their students, more aware of their cultures and feelings, and more sensitive to their needs.

Researching the Contributions of Women and Ethnic Minorities. Besides lacking knowledge about the cultures of ethnic minority groups, many TAs have done little research on the contributions by these groups to specific disciplines. Contributions made by women are also likely to have been ignored in previous disciplinary research. Since the accomplishments of minorities and women have not been well documented, it often takes vigorous inquiry to supplement the scholarship that has already been established in an area. In addition to new knowledge, alternative paradigms of thinking may be generated by such inquiry (see Belenky and others, 1987). This kind of research is necessary for a TA who is intent on enriching the curriculum in a given field with diversity in mind.

Uncovering One's Own Biases. Biases are often very subtle and deep-seated, but they can surface in inadvertent remarks and behavior that will offend students from ethnic minority groups, students with disabilities, gay and lesbian students, and returning adults. Participating in workshops designed to increase self-awareness and uncover racial, ethnic, and sexual stereotypes or reading about common myths and perceptions are activities useful for helping TAs to develop the sensitivity they need to teach a diverse student body.

Learning About Bias in Instructional Materials. TAs should understand how biased instructional material can inhibit the learning of nontraditional students, perpetuate stereotypes, and limit the curriculum. They should carefully evaluate textbooks for racially or sexually offensive material or for omission of references to the contributions of women and ethnic minorities. It may be necessary to prepare supplemental materials to use with existing texts. TAs should become aware of how tests can be biased against nontraditional students, and they should be able to interpret test scores with this knowledge in mind.

Learning About Campus Resources for Nontraditional Students. Teaching assistants should expend some effort learning about the different resources available to nontraditional students on campus. Such information will help TAs advise and refer students and obtain the help that they themselves may need for teaching minority students well.

Conclusions

Teaching nontraditional students is an important activity. It deserves special effort and requires additional thought, knowledge, and preparation from the professors of the future. The goal—to make the institution more responsive to students' diversity—must be understood and taken seriously. To be responsive requires the ability to motivate and inspire students to do their best. Achievement—measured by grades and accumulation of course credit—occurs in the classroom. Although extracurricular activities and settings contribute to students' comfort and development, in-class success is what earns the degree that proves success and can lead to a fulfilling career. Teaching, then, remains at the heart of nontraditional students' success.

Those who are preparing to teach must examine their own attitudes and ask themselves whether they truly want to ensure the success of nontraditional students. Future faculty members must be willing to question their own methods, instead of attributing learning difficulties to students' deficiencies alone. They must be willing to be more conscious about their teaching than many of their predecessors have been, and they must be willing to work hard to compensate for past omissions.

Teaching will not necessarily succeed just because it is based on subject matter; rather, knowledge about motivation and aspiration is at the heart of successful educational programs. Faculty members of the future who are aware of these factors and who work to teach well will help all students, traditional and nontraditional alike, to reap the benefits.

References

Anderson, J. A. "Cognitive Styles and Multicultural Populations." *Journal of Teacher Education*, 1988, *39* (1), 2-9.

Astin, A. *Preventing Students from Dropping Out.* San Francisco: Jossey-Bass, 1975.

Banks, J. A. *Multiethnic Education: Theory and Practice.* Newton, Mass.: Allyn & Bacon, 1988.

Belenky, M., and others. *Women's Ways of Knowing: The Development of Self, Voice, and Mind.* New York: Basic Books, 1987.

Crumpbacker, L., and Vander Haegen, E. *Integrating the Curriculum: Teaching About Lesbians and Homophobia.* Working paper no. 138. Wellesley, Mass.: Center for Research on Women, Wellesley College, 1984.

Green, M. F. (ed.). *Minorities on Campus: A Handbook for Enhancing Diversity.* Washington, D.C.: American Council on Education, 1988.

Hall, R. M., and Sandler, B. R. *The Classroom Climate: A Chilly One for Women?* Washington, D.C.: Association of American Colleges, 1982.

Hammill, D., Leigh, J., McNutt, G., and Larsen, S. "Defining Disabilities." *Learning Disability Quarterly*, 1981, *3*, 1.

Hilliard, A. G. "Teachers and Cultural Styles in a Pluralistic Society." In *NEA Today*, Washington, D.C.: National Education Association, 1989.

Kuroiwa, P. "The 'Invisible' Students." *Momentum*, 1975, *63*, 34-36.

Marienau, C., and Chickering, A. W. "Adult Development and Learning." In B. Menson (ed.), *Building on Experiences in Adult Development.* New Directions for Experiential Learning, no. 16. San Francisco: Jossey-Bass, 1982.

Pemberton, G. *On Teaching the Minority Student: Problems and Strategies.* Brunswick, Me.: Bowdoin College, 1988.

Sedlacek, W. E. "Teaching Minority Students." In J. H. Cones III, J. F. Noonan, and D. Janha (eds.), *Teaching Minority Students.* New Directions for Teaching and Learning, no. 16. San Francisco: Jossey-Bass, 1983.

Nancy Van Note Chism is program director for faculty and TA development, Center for Teaching Excellence, Ohio State University.

Jamie Cano is assistant professor of agricultural education, Ohio State University. He is involved in the Hispanic Task Force Committee at the university and teaches a course on multicultural education.

Anne S. Pruitt is director of the Center for Teaching Excellence, Ohio State University. She has written extensively on the subject of ethnic minorities in higher education.

Graduate faculty members fill several demanding roles as they assist TAs' progress through three stages of development.

TA Supervision

Jo Sprague, Jody D. Nyquist

Few faculty members set as a career goal the supervision of graduate teaching assistants (TAs). Typically, a faculty member volunteers or is drafted into such a position. For instance, Professor A has a primary investment in the teaching of Economics 208. The content of the course deals with the fundamentals that she mastered years ago, and she loves the performance aspects of the large lecture class of 750 students. In addition, by taking on this major responsibility for the department, her load is lightened one quarter a year, thus freeing substantial blocks of time for conducting her own research. This large class requires the assistance of fifteen TAs, who each meet two lab sections weekly. As an element of teaching this course, Professor A has the responsibility to supervise these TAs.

Professor B, in contrast, has a vision of how beginning university students can best learn expository writing skills. His teaching approach is fully elaborated in his popular introductory text. Rather than teaching just twenty-five freshmen a quarter, he serves as coordinator of all the sections of composition taught by thirty TAs. In this role, he is able to guide an important aspect of his department's curriculum and to keep in touch with students' responses, useful in revising his textbook.

Professor C has still another reason for supervising TAs. She is a physicist who has physics education as her foremost interest. She attends conferences and conducts research related to physics pedagogy. She is interested in the recruitment, education, and development of physics teachers and professors. She teaches a proseminar for all the new TAs in her department and serves as a resource person for those who are assisting professors and for those few who have been assigned to teach their own sections of basic courses. In her view, a very important part of her professional identity is her involvement in helping TAs become effective university teachers.

We could go on to Professor D, who is an assistant professor new to the campus, and who, at the chair's request, is now saddled with a job nobody in the department wants; or to Professor E, who is burned out on teaching and wants to get out of the classroom; or to Professor F, who sees TA supervision as a good way to recruit graduate students to study with him. Obviously, professors find themselves in the role of supervising TAs for varying reasons, with varying levels of commitment, and varying preparation for the role. Whatever the case, TA supervisors accept responsibility for overseeing the work and professional development of one or more TAs.

This chapter examines the complexity of such a responsibility. First, because the TA supervisor role has not been fully described, we explore the major dimensions of that role. Fulfilling the role will depend in part on the level of experience and sophistication of the TAs being supervised. We argue, therefore, that by analyzing how TAs typically develop as teachers, we can trace their professional advancement through three rather predictable phases. We also examine the implications of this progression in terms of what constitutes appropriate supervisory relationships and behavior at each phase. Finally, we offer our concept of the ideal circumstances under which TA supervision ought to occur.

Components of the TA Supervisor's Role

Whatever their reasons for getting involved in supervision, TA supervisors play multiple roles. At a minimum, a supervisor must function as a manager of a group of employees, as an educator modeling the teaching of undergraduates, and as a mentor for the TAs. Each role entails a specialized set of leadership skills.

TA Supervisors as Managers. The TA, although primarily a graduate student, is nevertheless an employee. It follows that the supervisor, although primarily a professor, is inevitably a personnel manager. Management tasks include setting minimal standards for instruction, determining whether TAs are meeting those standards, and, if necessary, removing TAs who are not meeting the needs of undergraduate students. These activities all occur in relation to students' satisfactory progress as graduate students, as well as in terms of their apprenticeship or employment as beginning instructors in a department.

For many TA supervisors, these managerial tasks are dimensions of a role for which they are neither philosophically nor practically prepared. Academics often do not like to have managerial models applied to any aspect of their professional careers. Departmental chairs, for example, tend to reject comparisons of themselves to bosses or managers. In academic environments, professors do not manage or supervise their colleagues but very carefully respect the academic freedom and autonomy of their colleagues. For the TA supervisor, a similar distaste for management concepts may take the form of a reluctance to require TAs, as colleagues in training, to attend regular staff meetings, adhere to standard formats, or document their performance. In academia, it may seem intrusive and disrespectful to engage in supervisory behaviors that would be accepted unquestioningly in other organizational settings.

Moreover, most faculty members are not only uncomfortable with management tasks but also have virtually no experience with personnel management. They manage their own classes, their time, their money, and their relationships, but they have not had to hire, motivate, appraise, reward, discipline, or dismiss other adults in a work setting. Professors may grade their students, but they do not fire them for poor performance. They may ask a departmental secretary to redo a piece of work, but they do not determine that person's work schedule. Although faculty members participate in the anonymous, confidential, and mysterious rites of peer review, most have never experienced anything like a formal employment appraisal.

Neither discomfort with management concepts nor inexperience with management tasks can erase the fact that any supervisor of a large or multisection course is, in a very real sense, a manager. Adjusting to the idea of the role seems to be the most formidable step. Mastery of a handful of basic management techniques is not difficult. Management literature suggests some simple but important axioms that, when followed, can help a supervisor coordinate the work of a group of TAs.

Good managers spend a great deal of time on planning, and they plan far ahead. Coordinators of large or multisection courses face the necessity of selecting texts, scheduling lecture topics, designing assignments, and preparing examinations far in advance. When working with a team, a faculty member loses some of the luxuries of spontaneous adaptation. Problems with this aspect of the managerial role go beyond time management. One of the most difficult cognitive shifts for people first assuming any sort of management position is to see planning as a primary form of work. They feel that they are not producing when they are planning, yet the mental work of formulating goals, allocating tasks, setting priorities, and anticipating contingencies is precisely what management is about. Once academics embrace the notion of management as a conceptual puzzle requiring mental work, rather than as a pedestrian bureaucratic task, their academic predispositions are tapped. We observe that if supervising professors become intellectually engaged by the challenges of course management, they solve intricate instructional problems and design elegant course structures, often far more creatively than managers do in other organizations.

Good managers are visible and accessible. A popular concept that seems to evoke a positive response from undergraduates is "management by walking around." Students' evaluations repeatedly include comments about the value of having supervisors visit labs, quiz sections, and tutorials. Such visibility and informal availability seem to communicate that both the professor and the department care about the course and the undergraduates. Like the students being taught, the TAs being supervised prefer a supervisor whose presence is felt on a daily basis.

Good managers keep their people informed. One of the main complaints we hear from TAs echoes that of members of other organizations: They claim that the NETMA (nobody ever tells me anything) factor has kept them from being effective TAs. They feel embarrassed and unhelpful when students ask them questions they cannot answer, particularly questions about course assignments, deadlines, and policies. As members of the instructional team, TAs need accurate and timely information.

Good managers are collaborative and open to feedback. Organizational scholars continue to confirm the effectiveness of participative approaches to management in contrast to autocratic, top-down styles. The particular applications of collaborative organizational principles to TA supervision have been justified on both pragmatic and philosophical grounds (Wilson and Stearns, 1985). Good decisions require good information, and TAs are on the academic front line, closest to the best data on what is and is not working in a class. Further, seeking TAs' opinions about how best to approach instructional problems in a course also ensures their commitment to carry through various approaches and strategies. Even if the issue of management effectiveness were put aside, nowhere would this collaborative orientation seem to be more appropriate than in a community of scholars, committed to a spirit of problem solving though inquiry.

Good managers make their expectations clear. To be successful, TAs need to be told what is expected of them. It seems that supervisors often assume that TAs know what their job is, and that it would be insulting to spell it out. Nevertheless, beginning graduate students are not likely to have the same intuitive, natural responses to solving instructional problems that a seasoned instructor demonstrates. Their uncertainties are compounded when they come to a department from other universities, or even from other countries, where academic practices may be very different. New TAs especially need an explicit orientation to the particular role they are asked to play in a course. They need answers to their questions: What are we expected to do in quiz sections? Are we to answer questions, or are we to structure formal reviews or present supplementary lectures? How many office hours are we to hold? When are homework assignments, papers, and exams to be returned? What does it mean to comment on students' papers? What kinds of test items are we to generate? How should undergraduates study for a final? If TAs are new to campus or new to teaching, they may also be unaware of institutional policies regarding sexual harassment, academic dishonesty, course attendance, and grading.

Good managers give regular feedback. People need to know how they are doing, even when that information is not good news. Their energies can then be directed toward improving their performance, rather than toward trying to read a supervisor's mind. Morale and productivity are both related to regular and specific feedback. Unfortunately, however, most TAs are not aware of how their work is evaluated. Again, because most professors have never conducted performance appraisals, evaluation seems difficult. An added complexity is that TAs may be doing quite well as students in graduate courses but may be struggling as TAs, and vice versa. The TA supervisor must provide clear and explicit feedback on the performance of TAs in regard to instructional responsibility.

Good managers balance task orientations and relational orientations. TAs work most effectively when they know what to do, but they also work well when they have a sense of community. The research on TA socialization reported in Chapter Two reveals that feelings of identification hinge on interpersonal relationships, peer support systems, and inclusion in group social activities. Effective supervisors are frequently the ones who take the time to create a warm and supportive social climate and to make each TA feel welcome. Effective management, however, is only one aspect of the TA supervisor's responsibility. Beyond the important aspects of management lies the responsibility of modeling effective professorial behavior.

TA Supervisors as Professorial Models. The role of professorial model for TAs is not always fully recognized by faculty members who teach undergraduate courses with the assistance of TAs. The first responsibility of TA supervisors, of course, is to teach the students enrolled in their classes. Setting the goals of instruction, deciding the quality of the educational experience that students should have, determining how a course fits into an overall curriculum, establishing basic course policies, protecting students' basic rights—these are all responsibilities of the course supervisor. Supervisors must delegate tasks judiciously and collaborate with their TAs, but they must still remember that they themselves bear ultimate responsibility.

A major student complaint in multisection undergraduate courses centers on the issue of consistency. Students report that different quiz sections cover different material, require widely varying amounts of work, and employ inconsistent evaluation practices. New graduate students probably will not know the purpose of a course, how it fits into the departmental and university curriculum, and how it fits into the students' lives. Supervisors are challenged, first to establish a vision of the goals of instruction and then to generate a commitment to working with TAs to achieve those outcomes. Before instruction begins, the TAs and the supervisor should have a shared answer to the question "How do we want students to be different as a result of this course?" This clear sense of educational mission will help TAs understand course policies. It will give them some reference point for making decisions when unexpected situations arise.

The positions taken by TA supervisors reflect their teaching philosophies, values, and general approaches to the art of teaching. For TAs who observe the seriousness of a faculty member's commitment to quality instruction, the supervisor takes on the important role of educational model. Shulman (1989) has commented on the significance of each student's observational apprenticeship. Basically, he means that students learn—both negatively and positively, both consciously and unconsciously—from the models they observe. TAs develop assumptions about educational goals, teacher-student relationships, grading and evaluation systems, and teaching methods from these observations. A primary professional role for TA supervisors, then, is to serve as effective instructional models.

The best role models do not produce clones of themselves; rather, they take the time to think aloud about the steps that have gone into their decisions. New TAs do need to hear good lectures, make copies of excellent handouts, and collect classroom exercises. More than that, however, those who are continuing in academic careers need to learn how to prepare a lecture, select a text, and choose a grading system. The best models are those who can talk about the inner work of teaching, the cognitive steps that precede action. They can talk about the changes they make and the options they have considered and rejected. Insights gained from such models are more generalizable than insights gained through direct imitation.

Good role models illustrate the complexity and tensions of teaching. Even though experienced teachers may appear confident and assured on the surface, aspiring teachers need to hear about all the indecision, the weighing, and the shifting that may often be going on underneath. Usually there is no best decision, just one that represents a balance of present factors. Teachers make mistakes, have doubts and regrets, and question their own priorities and motivations. By showing new teachers that there is vulnerability, pain, and ambiguity in this life they have chosen, senior colleagues also introduce TAs to the excitement and opportunities of teaching.

TA Supervisors as Mentors. Mentorship is one of our most important professional responsibilities, especially with the need to add 500,000 people to our ranks by the year 2000. Most graduate students report having attended graduate school because of encouragement from undergraduate professors. Similarly, most professors choose academia because of encouragement from professors at the graduate level. Graduate faculty know the satisfactions of participating in the development of new research scholars, moving talented students through the mastery of content and research tools, and watching them develop into confident and original thinkers. The same pride and fulfillment can reward participation in the emergence of a fine teaching professor. Mentoring the next generation of professors, especially minority members, is a high calling and a serious responsibility.

Each of these supervisory roles—manager, educational role model, and professional mentor—requires certain skills. Even when the TA supervisor does well in all three roles, however, work with TAs does not always progress smoothly. Effective TAs are not created overnight; they develop over time. The most successful TA supervisors understand that beginning teachers go through a developmental process and recognize that their supervision must change at each stage of this development.

Understanding TAs from a Developmental Perspective

Research on the ways in which faculty members develop indicates that there are shifts over time in what instructors are concerned about (Fuller, 1969; Book and Eisenberg, 1979) and in the kinds of vocabulary they use to talk about their disciplines (Williams, in press). Kagan (1988) summarizes findings from a number of studies which suggest characteristic changes that occur as teachers and counselors become more effective in their roles. On the basis of Stoltenberg's (1981) model, we suggest that TAs undergo similar development along the same dimensions. TAs tend to move from feeling overwhelmed to feeling more confident, from having limited awareness to having expanded awareness of their impact on others, from relying on single frameworks to recognizing the value of using many frameworks, and from having a weak sense of professional identity to having a strong one.

As TAs change and evolve, three different labels seem to describe the phases experienced by at least those who are headed toward academic careers. The beginning TA may be seen as a *senior learner* who is more sophisticated and motivated than most undergraduate students but whose primary academic success so far has been in the role of learner. After a period of initiation, as the TA's self-concept has "crossed over" and the teaching role has become at least somewhat internalized, the term *colleague in training* tends to fit. More experienced TAs, who have developed substantial instructional skills and demonstrated sound judgment, come to be seen as *junior colleagues*. These three designations of the roles that TAs play seem to capture the sense of progression that occurs during an apprenticeship. Roughly sorting the TAs one supervises into these three levels is a useful exercise, since the labels themselves imply relationships and needs. Positing these three stages of TA development invites a detailed analysis of how teaching assistants typically think, behave, and interact in each phase.

TAs as Senior Learners. TAs are selected because they are expert students, and that is the role they play comfortably and well. Suddenly becoming teachers or instructors, usually just months after the end of their own undergraduate experience, they tend to identify more with the students in their classes than with the instructors they are assisting. For most TAs, this is a troubling and confusing transition. They start out their assignments worried about whether they fit at all into an instructional role: Can I really do this? Do I look like a teacher? What will I wear? What will the students call me? A great deal of their energy goes into such personal concerns. The newest TAs are not yet confident of their mastery of subject matter. They tend, for example, to use the language of their disciplines in somewhat imprecise and unsophisticated ways. Moreover, since they are unfamiliar with the basic rules of instruction and the norms of the academy, they are understandably overwhelmed by teaching. They may feel like outsiders. To compensate, they are quick to use a single intellectual framework to inform their teaching and to use a single educational model to guide their practice.

TAs as Colleagues in Training. As TAs settle into the new role, they become more concerned about their lack of teaching skills. Their confidence as teachers advances along with their insights into their personal impact and their openness to exploring alternative instructional approaches. Even as the sense of professional identity starts to emerge, however, there is still a tendency for TAs to measure their own performance against idealized models. As they progress, TAs tend less to duplicate the techniques of charismatic professors or to transfer others' ideas directly to their own classes. They begin to adapt teaching methods to their own personal styles and to figure out unique solutions to novel problems. The need to appear professional also shows up in TAs' vocabulary during this phase. They are likely to become immersed in the specialized jargon and rarified methodological debates of their chosen disciplines. Unless a supervisor makes clear what is happening during the middle stage of a TA's development, the TA may overwhelm undergraduates by using recently acquired technical language and abstract conceptualizations. This is a signal that professionalism is developing, but perhaps at the expense of undergraduate students.

TAs as Junior Colleagues. During the latter stages of development, if all has gone well, TAs' general focus is outward, and their intellectual processes are integrative. No longer so worried about assuming new roles or mastering skills, their primary concerns involve discovering ways to help students learn. At this point, TAs need opportunities to make professional judgments and try out creative educational approaches. They can tell when an approach is working and can make adjustments if it is not. A well-differentiated and highly personal set of educational frameworks guides them. TAs are able to transcend, combine, and create systems of instruction and to express their academic knowledge in a variety of vocabularies. They feel increasingly confident of their skills and their professional identity. They have learned to communicate in collegial ways. In short, they are just the people we would all like to hire as assistant professors.

These developmental phases must be recognized and considered if our training programs are to meet the needs of the constantly developing TA. A carefully designed program for the supervision and education of TAs can help them progress through these stages rapidly and smoothly. Most important, such a program can ensure that all talented and motivated graduate students do arrive at the level of valued junior colleague and do not stall or become fossilized at some intermediate stage.

Implications of TAs' Developmental Phases for Supervision

Recognizing that the characteristics and needs of teaching assistants evolve over time, supervisors can adjust their leadership accordingly. For instance, although the roles of manager, educational role model, and professional mentor are important throughout an apprenticeship, the relative emphasis of these roles changes and reconfigures as the TA advances. Such an adaptive orientation is consistent with literature that links leadership effectiveness with the ability of leaders to adjust their behavior to the maturity of those they are leading (see Hersey and Blanchard, 1982). Individuals who are new to a task need close supervision, a great deal of task direction, and personal support. As followers develop skill and confidence, good leadership becomes less and less directive. At the stage of their highest maturity, followers can be granted a wide range of autonomy. The leader's role recedes to that of consultant and resource.

For a TA supervisor, one of the most direct uses of this orientation would be through progressive delegation. Delegating educational responsibility is a matter of great ambivalence for most supervisors, who may tend to view it as an all-or-nothing process. Instead, however, they can think of delegation as a gradual transfer of responsibility that occurs in stages: "Do this task my way, and check back with me." "Think about this problem, generate a few best options, and discuss them with me." "You select the option, but check with me before you proceed." "Make the decision, but let me know if you have problems or if you encounter anything we have never discussed." The notions of adaptive leadership and progressive delegation can be helpful to a TA supervisor who is thinking about ways to relate to a varied group of graduate students. Table 1 suggests some of the dimensions of change that may occur as supervisors design programs to optimize TAs' development. The most productive relationship between a supervisor and a TA probably differs according to whether the graduate student is at the level of senior learner, colleague in training, or junior colleague.

Supervision of TAs as Senior Learners. When TAs are first appointed, they are more aware of having a job than of entering a profession. Many TAs do not know whether they will become professors or make some other application of their advanced studies. Continuing their graduate education is their primary concern, and a teaching assistantship is a means to do that. Their immediate need is to know exactly what is expected of them to retain the assistantship. As a result, the initial interaction of supervisors and TAs emphasizes the role of the supervisor as personnel manager. We also know that new TAs are mostly concerned about whether they will fit into the role of teacher. To relieve this anxiety, a supervisor can create an environment where people feel free to ask questions, however trivial they may seem.

The teaching assignments of new TAs ought to build on their strengths as students and ease the transition into the instructional role. Assisting with the administrative chores of a large lecture class helps TAs see how much work and planning go into balancing the academic and logistical elements of teaching. Tutoring, holding office hours, and managing carefully planned quiz sections allow TAs to practice giving clear explanations of concepts and to capitalize on the recency of their own first encounters with the material. At the same time, such focused interactions with learners move TAs toward an advanced level of discourse within their disciplines by showing them the need for precision of language and conceptual clarity. Involving new TAs in grading and testing helps them think about the complex issues of evaluation. In the practical context of deciding what is a right answer or a good paper, they will discover that success depends on what one is trying to teach.

At this point, two-way interaction becomes essential. After a few weeks, meetings with a course supervisor and other TAs should begin to move away from an emphasis on what to do and toward faculty-led discussions of why something is done this way in this course, as well as toward interactive dialogues on the pros and cons of the approach. The sessions change in tone, from briefings to staff meetings. The manage-

Table 1. Program Design Implications of the
Three Phases of TA Development

	Senior Learner	Colleague in Training	Junior Colleague
Relative emphasis in supervisor's role	Manager	Educational model	Mentor
Teaching assignment	Assist professor Grade papers Hold office hours	Take larger role in course, some lecturing, etc. Teach own section of a course	Take primary responsibility for course design Assist professor with advanced course
Teacher-training activity	Orientation Briefing	Proseminar designed to build repertoire of teaching skills	Reflective practicum
Relationship with other TAs	As co-learners As support system	As colleagues As resources	As senior TA assisting with orientation of new TAs
Function of evaluation	Assess performance in initial teaching assignments	Provide feedback on instructional skills	Provide feedback on developing a personal teaching style Learn collegial ways of giving and receiving feedback

ment style becomes increasingly collaborative, but the meetings still center on the successful functioning of the current course.

Peer interactions are also crucial for beginning TAs at these early stages. TAs need to receive support and reassurance as they adjust to the teaching role. One of the best services a supervisor can provide is to facilitate this sort of communication among new TAs and between the beginning and advanced groups of TAs.

The supervisor's evaluative role should take two forms at this stage. First, feedback on the TA as employee must be very clear and explicit: "You are to have five office hours a week, and I see only three posted." Second, feedback on instructional effectiveness can deal with the global topic of adjustment to the role. The feedback may address such issues as whether the TA seems to feel comfortable in the role, is starting to think the way a teacher does, relates appropriately to students, projects a professional image, and the like.

Supervision of TAs as Colleagues in Training. During the next phase of professional development, when TAs have begun to feel secure in their roles as employees and have started to see themselves as an important part of the educational process, the bulk of their learning takes place. The second column of Table 1 highlights the training-design implications of this phase. TAs' firsthand experiences with instruction will motivate them to develop new teaching skills. As TAs seek guidance about teaching, their relationships with their supervisors change. Supervisors are able to function less as employment managers and more as role models. Their primary tasks include offering a variety of instructional models, increasing TAs' exposure to educational frameworks for analysis, and most important, giving TAs the opportunity to build a repertoire of teaching skills through direct practice.

After a term or so, most TAs are ready for more responsibility. In a large class, the TA can be asked to present a few lectures, make more sophisticated evaluations, or design test items and assignments with the approval of the supervisor. If TAs are assigned to their own quiz sections or even to their own courses at this stage of development, they should not be expected to make major decisions about course design; they are not yet sufficiently aware of the implications of various choices, the possible contradictions among course elements, or even the norms for students' work in certain departments. Because of its complexity, overall course design is generally best left to senior faculty members, with TAs given progressively more freedom to elaborate on set units or assignments. As colleagues in training, TAs are occupied with mastering the skills of lecturing, leading discussions, and grading papers, and they should be able to practice these skills in course frameworks that have been designed for their success.

One issue that may arise at this phase centers on the degree of TAs' autonomy in a given course structure. As TAs become more confident and begin to explore other frameworks and personalize their teaching styles, those who are most enthusiastic about teaching may suggest innovations. Supervisors must make decisions about such suggestions according to the quality of instruction sought for the undergraduates in a course. Is the idea consistent with course goals? Has the TA thought it through carefully? Does the TA have the skill to handle a new technique? If the answers to these questions are affirmative, it may be a good idea to try out the new approach and have TAs as a group compare its effectiveness to other approaches. If a suggestion is ill advised, a supervisor can find tactful ways to reinforce initiative and creativity while still firmly vetoing the idea. At this point, it is crucial for the supervisor to place the decision in the context of the immediate course; for example, take-home exams, required field trips, or peer grading may be inappropriate to a specific course. Supervisors and TAs can explore the ways in which these same educational strategies can be effective in meeting academic objectives of other courses the TAs may teach later.

Training activities during the second phase of TAs' development typically emphasize building a repertoire of teaching skills and developing a set of principles to guide the selection of strategies. This is the ideal time for a professional seminar (given for academic credit, if possible) that explores issues of teaching and learning in one's own discipline. The design of such a course is a challenge. A graduate TA is involved in learning the vocabulary and methodologies of a discipline but is simultaneously expected to master the vocabulary and models of teaching. She or he is involved in becoming, for instance, a professional chemist and a chemistry professor at the same time. Generic educational models will seem neither interesting nor valuable unless the supervisor relates them to the context of the discipline. The supervisor serves as an intellectual bridge—selecting, adapting, and customizing those pedagogical models that really illuminate how learning is facilitated in each particular course. Besides providing TAs with a few well-chosen frameworks to apply to their teaching, such proseminar experiences should have a strong training component that emphasizes particular instructional skills, such as lecturing, leading discussions, writing test items, and responding to students' work.

During the intermediate stages of TAs' development, supervisors can try to facilitate a shift in the way TAs relate to their peers. They are more than co-learners and supportive friends. The notion emerges of a professional colleague, one who shares a level of specialized training and commitment to a code of ethics. TAs who are not yet in a position to think of their professors as colleagues can learn to work with their peers in collegial ways. They may observe each other in the classroom, review one another's lecture outlines, share teaching resources, collaborate on test construction, and discuss alternative philosophies of teaching.

Evaluation of TAs at this phase should emphasize the appraisal of teaching skills from multiple perspectives, using multiple measures. To enhance their confidence in their teaching and build their awareness of their impact as teachers, TAs need feedback from students, peers, and observers. Supervisors can introduce videotaping, systematic observation, near-verbatim transcriptions, and class interviews, as well as the usual ratings from students and observations by supervisors. The TA should not be looking for an overall rating as a "good" teacher or a "poor" teacher. Evaluation should center on gathering information about many perceptions of TAs' teaching behavior, analyzing that information in terms of specific goals, and designing strategies for change. When the TA sets a personal goal for change, he or she may invite the supervisor or another observer to enter into a coaching role (Nyquist and Wulff, 1982).

Supervision of TAs as Junior Colleagues. In the latter stages of his or her teaching assistantship, a graduate student may seem like a junior colleague who no longer requires supervision. The supervisor's role remains crucial, though, because at this stage of development TAs learn about collegial relationships. Graduate students can be helped to move from seeing themselves as competent teachers to seeing themselves as professors who shape and define disciplines. The third column of Table 1 outlines the form this relationship may take. A supervisor's evaluations of junior colleagues should approximate the kinds of supportive but honest interactions that would ideally characterize collegial communication. Although the supervisor's roles as manager and role model remain in the picture, the role of mentor is emphasized at this stage.

Teaching assignments may include opportunities to be involved in course design and make professional judgments, and TAs may be given the chance to teach more challenging courses. Their professional experiences can be enhanced by some involvement in course administration and by service as senior TAs. Just as there is truth in the maxim that one never really understands a subject until one teaches it, so it seems that one of the best ways to consolidate what one knows about teaching is to help a beginning teacher learn about it. With basic skills well in hand and a personal teaching style emerging, the TA is now in a position to discuss matters of professional judgment, overall instructional strategy, and educational priorities.

The formal teacher-training activities at this advanced level can best be designed as what Schön (1987) refers to as the "reflective practicum." This is a case-oriented session that helps the professional in training become a more critical and reflective problem solver. The topics raised will force the TA to combine intellectual models and redefine systems to solve novel problems. In a practicum with other reflective practitioners, TAs gain experience in articulating and supporting their positions on pedagogical issues. Such dialogues help TAs move out of the student role and prepare to assume their professorial roles, in which they will be expected to communicate simply, directly, and precisely.

An Ideal of TA Supervision

The approach to supervision that we have outlined requires the TA supervisor to master three difficult and demanding roles and then to individualize and adjust supervisory activities according to close observations of the development of TAs throughout their apprenticeship. Conceived in this way, the task of preparing TAs to become effective teachers (in addition to able researchers) probably takes more time and effort than any single TA supervisor has. TA supervision fits into the larger context of the university, of course, and other units of the institution can assist with this process. In envisioning an ideal scenario for TA supervision, we can start with the departmental chair or the department faculty as a whole.

We will assume that the departmental chair understands the significance of the large lecture and multisection courses a TA supervisor is to teach or supervise. We will also assume that the chair has managed to give the TA supervisor released time. In addition, we assume that the TA supervisor has been given enough TAs for the large lecture courses, as well as readers, so that students' writing can be used as a learning tool. Thus, the large courses and multisection courses are adequately staffed.

Adequate staffing requires adequately trained TAs. Even if our TA supervisor were prepared to manage, provide educational leadership, and act as mentor, the TAs would still need sustained, direct instruction about their roles. They could get it through a combined universitywide and departmental orientation in the fall, followed by a quarter- or semester-long professional seminar taught by one of the senior members of the department who is interested in the teaching of the discipline. The orientation would take the entire week before classes began and would be the prime method for socializing TAs into their new responsibilities, thus initiating their transition from senior learners to colleagues in training. A proseminar (a graduate seminar meeting once a week, with appropriate readings and in-class experiences)would explore the philosophy, theory, and practice of teaching the discipline as TAs attempted to deal with these issues in their new positions as instructors of undergraduates. This seminar would be followed by continuous training, occurring each term that the TAs held their appointments (see Chapter Five for examples of such programs).

To assist with the orientation, the proseminar, and the ongoing training, the chair would select a senior TA, one planning to become a scholar and teacher. This person would have completed all Ph.D. coursework, would have passed comprehensive exams, and would currently be writing the dissertation. In addition, he or she would have experience in teaching the basic courses offered by the department. Given our understanding of the TA socialization process, as outlined in Chapter Two, this senior TA would be essential to the development of new TAs. This person would attend training sessions at the university's instructional development center for one term to be trained in microteaching and videocritiques, classroom observations, and classroom research techniques for collecting students' perceptions of TAs' effectiveness.

The senior TA would meet frequently with first-year TAs, TA supervisors, the chair of the department, and, of course, members of the university's instructional center, to ensure that TAs were progressing systematically through the stages of senior learner, colleague in training, and junior colleague. The senior TA would work individually with the beginning TAs, visiting classes, offering observations, and sharing resources. For the senior TA, this experience might be crucial in the decision to join the professoriate, as opposed to entering business, industry, or government.

To assist in these efforts, the ideal university would provides additional resources. An instructional center would adopt a consulting model meeting individually with professors and TAs from all departments to enhance instruction and address instructional issues and problems. The center would extend many services. A writing specialist would meet with TAs and teach them how to assist professors to construct clear writing assignments. TAs would be given practice and feedback on responding to students' papers and evaluating their writing. A course-evaluation specialist would collect students' perceptions of TAs' performance and consult with TAs about those findings. Instructional developers would provide classroom observations, instructional options, and recommendations. They would also locate and modify computer software and work with TAs to ensure effective use of computers for teaching many basic concepts. The staff of the instructional center would be available at no cost and would provide completely confidential consultations. They also would understand the developmental phases of TAs and would be able to furnish assistance at any of the stages.

We forgot to mention that our TA supervisor would be a well-known scholar, would still enjoy working with students just beginning to become interested in his or her discipline, and would just have won the all-university Distinguished Teaching Award. That is the ideal of what TA training could and should be. A fantasy? We hope not, and we know of several campuses that are currently approaching such an ideal. Obviously, a TA supervisor must work with whatever resources are available on his or her campus. Nevertheless, we believe that, even in the most limiting circumstances—TA supervisor plus TAs with no additional assistance—an understanding of the supervisor's roles of manager, professorial leader, and mentor will assist in preparing TAs for their responsibilities, both now and in the future. These roles depend, however, on the understanding of TAs' developmental levels. Taking a developmental approach to TA training allows the needs of TAs to be met much more effectively. Ensuring that the TA experience will be satisfying provides the best opportunity for recruiting outstanding young scholars to take their places as the next generation of professors.

References

Book, C. L., and Eisenberg, E. M. "Communication Concerns of Graduate and Undergraduate Teaching Assistants." Paper presented at the Speech Communication Association, San Antonio, Texas, 1979.

Fuller, F. F. "Concerns of Teachers: A Developmental Perspective." *American Educational Research Journal*, 1969, 2, 207–226.

Hersey, P., and Blanchard, K. *Management of Organizational Behavior.* (4th ed.) Englewood Cliffs, N.J.: Prentice-Hall, 1982.

Kagan, D. M. "Research on the Supervision of Counselors—and Teachers—in Training: Linking Two Bodies of Literature." *Review of Educational Research,* 1988, *58* (1), 1-24.

Nyquist, J. D., and Wulff, D. H. "The Use of Simultaneous Feedback to Alter Teaching Behaviors of University Instructors." *Journal of Classroom Interaction,* 1982, *18* (1), 11-17.

Schön, D. A. *Educating the Reflective Practitioner: Toward a New Design for Teaching and Learning in the Professions.* San Francisco: Jossey-Bass, 1987.

Shulman, L. S. "Toward a Pedagogy of Substance for Higher Education." Paper presented to the American Association for Higher Education, Chicago, April 3, 1989.

Stoltenberg, C. "Approaching Supervision from a Developmental Perspective: The Counselor Complexity Perspective." *Journal of Counseling Psychology,* 1981, *28* (1), 59-65.

Williams, J. M. "Two Metaphors for Cognitive Development." In E. Maimon (ed.), *Perspectives on Development.* Upper Montclair, N.J.: Boynton/Cook, in press.

Wilson, T., and Stearns, J. "Improving the Working Relationship Between Professor and TA." In J.D.W. Andrews (ed.), *Strengthening the Teaching Assistant Faculty.* New Directions for Teaching and Learning, no. 22. San Francisco: Jossey-Bass, 1985.

Jo Sprague is professor of Communication Studies, San Jose State University, where she supervises TAs in basic communication courses.

Jody D. Nyquist is a lecturer in the Department of Speech Communication and is director for instructional development at the Center for Instructional Development and Research, University of Washington.

Part 2.

Current Training Programs

Many different formats for TA training programs exist at institutions across the country, but all program formats need to respond to the same basic questions.

Designing Programs to Prepare TAs to Teach

Maryellen Weimer, Marilla D. Svinicki, Gabriele Bauer

As concern about the role and performance of teaching assistants (TAs) continues to grow, more and more universities find themselves initiating training programs or bolstering their present programs. As universities confront those tasks, a number of issues present themselves for consideration:

- Who should provide training?
- If there are different providers, what should be the relationships among them?
- What should be the program requirements and curricula?
- How long should the program be, and when should it occur?
- What sorts of follow-up activities should be offered?
- Do international TAs need separate and more extensive preparation?
- How should the effectiveness of training be evaluated?

Questions like these do not have "right" answers. It is more a case of reviewing the options, considering the roles and functions of TAs within the institution, examining the nature and climate of the university, and then making choices that take these various perspectives into account. The intent of this chapter is to help those designing or redesigning TA training programs, by reviewing various options. The goal is to consider the issues and describe some of the ways in which current programs handle them. To offer those perspectives, we have interviewed persons closely associated with TA training programs at fourteen universities across the country. (A list of the programs, as well as the names of persons interviewed, appears at the end of the chapter.) We do not claim any randomness or representativeness for the survey sample. We compiled the list on the basis of our knowledge and experience in this area. Those participating in the survey offered ample evidence, however, that the issues raised in the interviews were of concern to them. They, and those working with them, had considered and continue to consider these issues as they work to refine and further strengthen their efforts to prepare TAs for instructional responsibilities. The solutions they have found are often very innovative and institution-specific.

A word of caution to the reader: The programs are very fluid, since they respond to changes in the institutions. No one program, of course, is appropriate to all institutions, nor is a program at any given institution appropriate to all times or all departments. Even the very successful program constantly modifies its structure to meet the demands of its situation. Therefore, the program details included in this chapter are offered for inspiration, rather than as prescription. We hope you will find ideas that will suit your special needs or inspire you to adapt or design ideas of your own.

Who Should Provide Training?

Four possibilities come to mind. First, training can be offered by the instructional/faculty development unit of the university. Such units are staffed with persons who are knowledgeable about teaching and learning and who have experience working with instructors. Most also have at their disposal considerable resources and information related to effective teaching. Second, training can occur within the department to which a TA is assigned. Departments are particularly well situated to combine information about curricular content and teaching techniques. They know firsthand the nature of the content and the setting in which the instruction will occur. Third, more specialized training can occur at the level of a single course, and it frequently does if multiple sections of the course are being offered or if the course is large. All TAs who teach a particular course can work together with a course coordinator on teaching, content, assignments, and grading, an arrangement that tailors preparation to the situation. Fourth, training can be provided by the graduate school or by the college. Here, the advantages are related primarily to efficiency; one trainer can provide the needed instruction to a large group. If provided at the college level, training can still contain some degree of specialization.

Who most often provides the training in the programs surveyed? In virtually every case, training is given at more than one of these four levels. In some programs, the initial training (meaning an orientation to college teaching) is provided by the instructional or faculty development unit. Training at that level introduces TAs to college teaching and to the instructional policies and practices of the institution. It is followed by departmental training, where the focus is more on application of teaching techniques to curricular content. In some cases, the introduction to teaching is conducted by the graduate school, with application occurring at the departmental level, in terms of specific courses. A variety of other combinations also exist, but there is almost always more than one provider of training.

How Should Different Providers Relate to One Another?

How should these various providers relate to each other in order to maximize the effects of the training on the TAs' teaching? The concerns in this area involve issues of coordination, control, and interaction. Here, too, several different possibilities present themselves, although they are not so clearly differentiated as in the issue of providers. In one model, the instructional development unit coordinates efforts universitywide, providing support, consultation, and resources to the actual units in which the instruction occurs. Control of the program itself is decentralized, with decisions about the content and configuration of training made and implemented in the departments, which receive input, advice, and help from the instructional/faculty development unit. In this case, what usually evolves is a sort of partnership between the instructional/faculty development center and the department. Both providers work and make decisions together. In some cases, the instructional/faculty development unit provides general sessions (usually emphasizing pedagogy) in which departments require or strongly encourage their TAs to participate. In other cases, the instructional/faculty development unit makes actual presentations during the departmental training program or helps departments with instructional design, to ensure the proper balance of content and method in the departmental curriculum. In still other situations, the instructional/faculty development unit works with or for the department, implementing microteaching, videotaping, or consultation for the TAs.

In a second model, responsibility for preparing TAs occurs exclusively at the departmental level. Here, there is no expectation that the instructional development unit will coordinate the university's response to training needs. That unit may offer generic training, open to all TAs, or it may make resources and services known to departments, but departments use their own discretion about whether to avail themselves of these services. This decentralized model tends to result in a widely diverse departmental response to TAs' instructional needs. Some departments devote much time and energy to TAs' preparation; others devote virtually none.

It is possible to give the instructional/faculty development unit primary responsibility for preparing new TAs. In this third model, departments may contribute to those efforts, but when the instructional/faculty development unit assumes responsibility, any departmental training must meet certain basic criteria, as established by the unit. In this case, the entire training experience may occur outside the department.

In the programs we surveyed, the trends are not clear-cut. Many of the programs seem to combine the first and second models. In most of these cases, the instructional or faculty development units do not have a clear mandate to coordinate university efforts, but they seem rather to have fallen into that role. In some of these cases, there is a university mandate endorsing the training effort. Nevertheless, few instructional or faculty development units are in the position of having direct control over departmental efforts. One possible exception is the University of California at Los Angeles, where the instructional/faculty development unit funds departmental training activities, helping to ensure that all departmental programs include certain components. Most units are more in the position of making their resources and services known to departments and then working with departments, at the departments' request. In many cases, there has been a history of needing to persuade departments that preparation to teach ought to include more than knowledge of content.

Most of the programs surveyed report congenial relationships between instructional or faculty development units and departments, once such relationships have been established. The attempt is to cooperate, to support, and to integrate what at most universities is a variety of different activities. What does seem to be missing is interaction and support across different departmental providers. Many departments seem to operate in isolation, gaining help from an instructional/faculty development center if one exists but otherwise doing what they do quite independently and unaware of one another.

Despite their general lack of control, instructional or faculty development units have found some very creative ways of making themselves indispensable to training activities at the departmental level. The University of Colorado at Boulder, for example, has an instructional/faculty development unit that supervises the TA Coach Network, in which the unit trains and supports TAs who are selected and funded by departments, and who then function in the department as coaches to new TAs. At the University of California at Davis (UCD), departments are encouraged to develop proposals for retreats of two to three days, which address instructional issues of concern to TAs and faculty members. UCD's Teaching Resources Center then reviews these proposals and funds several.

This strategy encourages faculty and TAs to join in the exploration of instructional issues, an activity that the Teaching Resources Center sees as very instrumental in acclimating TAs to the particular cultures of the departments. Each spring, the University of Washington's Center for Instructional Development and Research conducts a planning meeting for departmentally appointed faculty members and senior TAs. The meeting is designed to provide information about instructional development resources available for TAs' training and to help the departmental representatives develop and refine plans for fall training activities in the departments.

The safest general conclusion about providers and their interrelationships would be that the locus of control for these programs is still very strongly at the department level. In the opinion of people we interviewed, little can be done about departments that do not take training activities seriously. Nevertheless, some instructional/faculty development units have found very creative ways of dealing with diversity. At Ohio State University, for example, the unit outlines three different options, which take the different levels and effectiveness of departmental training into account. Departments still choose how to have their TAs participate in the general orientation, but the unit advises them according to its knowledge of the departments' training.

What Should Be the Program Requirements and Curricula?

Two different questions related to program requirements and curricula seem to cause the most concern. Should participation in a training program be required? And who should participate?

Program Mandate. The first issue, mandatory attendance, has a number of different variations. The most basic form of the question, of course, is whether TAs should be required to attend at all. If not, should they be strongly encouraged, or should participation be entirely voluntary? If it is required, who does the requiring—the graduate school, the college or division, the department, or the university? If TAs are required to participate, concerns about remuneration quickly follow, particularly if participation is required above and beyond normal instructional hours. If TAs are paid, do they need any additional recognition, such as certificates or course credit? What if they are not paid?

Another aspect of attendance has to do with how much of the program is required. Are certain parts mandatory and others optional, or is attendance required but the choice of sessions left up to the participant?

A second requirement issue revolves around who should participate in these instructional activities. Should TAs with previous teaching experience be exempted? What about graduate students whose assistantships require only modest instructional activity, such as grading papers or conducting office hours or study sessions? A related concern is when TAs should participate in the training—before they begin teaching, at the same time they start teaching, or after a semester of experience?

The majority of the programs we surveyed do not require TAs to participate. At some places, however, there are such requirements. Some departments establish local requirements (in the case of Michigan State, a contract with the graduate student union requires training for all TAs). Even in the absence of hard-and-fast requirements, however, virtually everyone we interviewed emphasized that TAs' participation is strongly encouraged, generally at a variety of different levels. Moreover, according to reported levels of participation, the majority of TAs at these institutions participate voluntarily in activities designed to prepare them to teach.

Most of these institutions do not directly remunerate TAs for participation in these activities, although some do have clever ways of getting money to TAs, so that required participation before the semester begins will not cause financial difficulty. At Syracuse University, for example, the graduate student stipend was not increased when the training requirement was initiated. Rather than being paid in seventeen installments, TAs are now paid in eighteen installments, with the first payment made immediately after training ends but before the semester begins. Other universities remunerate in kind, making dormitory space and food available to participants. Those that do offer remuneration offer modest amounts, like fifty dollars for two full days of activity.

In a few cases, the decision of whether to remunerate TAs for participation is made at the departmental level. Some departments decide to pay and some do not. As one interviewee pointed out, "You then have TAs sitting side by side in general sessions, some being paid for their attendance and others not, which can cause some discomfort between them."

Several people in our interview sample did report certifying TAs' participation with some sort of diploma or certificate. At the University of Michigan, the departments of experienced TAs receive notification of the TAs' continued participation in follow-up instructional development programs. Several other programs indirectly reward TAs with awards for outstanding teaching. The University of Wyoming gives seven $1,000 awards annually to TAs on the basis of departmental nominations. At the University of Missouri, there is a cash prize for the TA who identifies an instructional problem and suggests the best solution. The problem and its solution are then described in materials distributed to all TAs.

Our interview subjects strongly believed that no graduate student should be exempted from training, and most do all they can to discourage exemptions. When pressed, however, almost all agreed that such training is really designed for graduate students new to college teaching and unfamiliar with a particular university. Training activities, they believe, would certainly benefit all graduate students, but most directly those who actually have instructional responsibilities.

Content. What should be the content of training? The question is less about options and more about degree. Basically, new college instructors need help in two areas: content and method. With respect to content, departments need to ensure consistency across different sections. Sometimes TAs need help learning content. More often, it is a matter of teaching pace and organization and ensuring uniformity of evaluative policies and practices. With respect to instructional strategies, training programs often include introductions to college teaching, with strong emphasis on practice. New TAs need to know how to lead discussions, stimulate students' participation, answer questions, and explain concepts in several ways. They need to know how to create climates conducive to learning and how to manage disruptive behavior. They need advice on working with students one-to-one in laboratory and office settings. They need help making the difficult transition from student to teacher, when they still occupy the student role.

Most of the people we interviewed provide training in both general areas, usually during orientation at the beginning of the year. A few universities include other topics in their orientations, such as sexual harassment, gender bias, university policies, practices relevant to teaching and students' conduct in the classroom, and instructional resources and services. Nevertheless, there are differences in degree of coverage, length of training, and methods used to deliver instruction. Most institutions use large lectures, workshops, and seminars, but there are differences in who does the presenting. Some rely on master teachers, speaking singly or on panels about topics primarily related to effective teaching techniques. Some use course coordinators who have experience working with TAs in instructional settings. Others rely on an instructional or faculty development staff, most of whose members are experienced workshop leaders who can offer a variety of resources, information, and ideas about teaching and learning. Still others rely on senior TAs, whose recent firsthand experience learning to teach at the institution gives them special credibility with fellow TAs. In fact, most programs incorporate experienced TAs at some point in initial training. A few bring in outside consultants to provide training.

People from institutions where orientation is provided by an instructional or faculty development unit emphasized the need to break down large instructional groups into smaller ones, so that new TAs have the opportunity to exchange ideas and raise issues of particular concern to them. Some form these groups according to type of teaching responsibility such as lab instructor, recitation leader, autonomous classroom instructor, occasional lecturer but full-time grader and course assistant.

Others divide groups along disciplinary lines. Still others construct cross-disciplinary groupings, to emphasize the aspects of teaching and learning that cross disciplinary lines.

A number of universities that offer general programs in which TAs from across the university participate let those TAs make some choice about what individual sessions they will attend. Syracuse University has the most elaborate of these choice models. TAs there preregister for sessions before orientation activities begin. Organizers there also ask TAs to indicate their degree of prior teaching experience and work, to ensure that some experienced TAs attend each session to act as resource persons.

How Long Should the Program Be and When Should It Occur?

The question of appropriate length is a good one, but it frequently gets changed to something like "How much time can we squeeze out for this activity?" Reality, rather than propriety, usually ends up dictating length. Even so, the programs represented in our survey do devote considerably different lengths of time to training activities, particularly in the orientation phase. At one extreme are places where orientation is confined to half a day. At the other extreme, training occurs eight hours a day for a full week. Most fall somewhere in the middle, with training occurring across two or three days, combining activities at the departmental level and general, universitywide programs. In most universities, some training continues at the departmental level throughout the first term or semester.

When should training occur? We do not have a definitive answer to that question. What we can report is when it typically occurs. In almost all the programs in our survey, training occurs just before or at the beginning of the first semester or term the TA is teaching. In a few isolated cases, instruction occurs weekly across the term of teaching responsibility. Many of the programs that begin with a general orientation, either alone or in combination with departmental activities, offer intermittent follow-up activities across the first term or semester; some even offer activities over the entire first year. In virtually all of these follow-up activities, however, participation is voluntary and drops off considerably after the initial activities.

What Sorts of Follow-Up Activities Should Be Offered?

Where training is highly decentralized, with most (if not all) training occurring at the departmental level, there is often no follow-up at that level, but TAs generally can participate in follow-up activities offered elsewhere in the university. The assumption of those we interviewed (and we certainly concur) is that initial training needs to be followed up, especially if it occurs before any teaching experience. It is truly in the classroom that the TA's skills are tested. In that context, questions are real, and the need for answers is often keenly felt. It is sometimes difficult to see the value of training without exposure to that real experience.

Activities that occur after initial training fall into several categories. First, some programs offer additional seminars, workshops, or programs that elaborate content introduced earlier, focus on application of content, or raise new issues (like academic integrity) that tend to emerge as the term progresses. In general, these programs are configured to offer the TA increased opportunities to interact, discuss, and respond. They are generally not large sessions but smaller, more intimate, personal exchanges.

Second, a number of programs offer as follow-up some sort of microteaching, videotape teaching experience, or peer observation. A few programs incorporate these activities as part of orientation. More offer this activity (and a few require it) as the term or semester progresses. The activities occur in a variety of different ways. Some are orchestrated by the department; far more are organized by the instructional/faculty development unit. In many cases, the consultant who reviews the videotape or does the in-class observation is a staff member who works for the instructional or faculty development unit. Some units place TAs in departments. Others use senior TAs to give new TAs feedback about their instruction. Most emphasize the importance of feedback to the TA, recognizing the inherent need to keep it formative and constructive. Most of the programs using feedback do not share assessments with anyone other than the TAs involved. At the University of Illinois at Urbana–Champaign, the Division of Instructional Development does report to departments on TAs who are dong an excellent job and on TAs who need more training. They believe telling a department about TAs who need further help prepares the department to respond to possible complaints and helps the department support TAs in their first teaching experiences.

Another common category of follow-up activities includes participation in some sort of student evaluation. Almost uniformly, such instructional evaluations are conducted early or at the midpoint of the first term or semester. In addition, most departments use standardized end-of-course evaluations. Many of those interviewed strongly emphasized the value of getting feedback to TAs early in their teaching experiences. Again, most disseminate results only to the TAs. All try to incorporate some sort of individual consultation about the results as part of the evaluative experience. The University of California at Davis, the University of Illinois, and the University of Washington also use formative evaluation, but in a unique format. The TA is strongly encouraged to let a facilitator come into the class for fifteen minutes, with the TA instructor absent, and interview students about their experiences in the class so far. These assessments are then summarized and discussed with the TA. This process is often referred to as small-group instructional diagnosis (SGID).

Many programs support and follow up initial training experiences with resource materials. Many have specifically prepared handbooks for TAs, which review institutional policies related to instruction and give more information and advice on teaching skills. Some publish newsletters for TAs. These may be produced once or twice a year, or two or three times a semester; many rely heavily on material contributed by TAs or senior faculty members. Some programs prepare and distribute bibliographies or prepare monographs relevant to the different instructional settings where TAs frequently teach (like labs or recitations). Still others have videotaped teaching samples available for review in the instructional or faculty development unit. Some prepare materials for those who work with TAs, such as course coordinators and TA consultants or peer observers. In all cases, these materials are used further to support and inform TAs' classroom activities. Specific examples of such materials are mentioned in Chapter Eleven.

Finally, most of the programs in our survey follow up by making consultation available to TAs. In general, these services are available upon request and provide a trained person (most often a staff member, although not always) to meet privately with TAs to discuss instructional issues of concern. In addition, consultants do in-class observations, review videotaped teaching samples, help decipher students' evaluations, review course materials, or put TAs in contact with other resources or information.

Not falling into any of these categories, but clearly worth mentioning, are minigrant programs. At Syracuse University, for instance, TAs and faculty members are encouraged to propose developmental teaching activities, which are funded from a central source, to encourage departmental improvement of instruction.

Do International TAs Need Separate and More Extensive Preparation?

The assumption behind this question rests on the fact that international TAs (ITAs), in addition to coping with their own inexperience in the classroom, must cope with teaching in a foreign language and with an education system very unlike the ones they have known. On many campuses, concerns initially raised about ITAs have led to a reckoning with the preparation of all new TAs.

Training for ITAs is both separate and more extensive in all the programs in our sample. The curriculum includes the same emphasis on content and method, but both are covered in more detail. In addition, language-speaking ability is typically assessed, and attempts are made to strengthen it. Activities in some of the programs address these special needs in very constructive ways. At the University of Missouri, for example, undergraduate students, in addition to experienced TAs and ITAs, are involved in efforts to prepare new ITAs. The new ITA presents a short lecture, which is taped. Undergraduate students act as an audience for the lecture and offer the ITA advice and suggestions. This seems a particularly good way of reinforcing the shared aspects of the educational endeavor. Students, too, are responsible for and contribute to classroom climates.

The programs in our survey do handle one issue differently: the integration of ITAs into normal training activities. Some do not integrate the two at any level. Others conduct special ITA training before orientation and then have the ITAs participate in the general training as well. In some cases, integration occurs at the departmental level, during or after orientation. A few institutions conduct the two trainings concurrently, with special and additional sessions required for ITAs. In most cases, whether the preparation is separate or integrated, language-skill training is provided by specialists in English as a Second Language (ESL). These and other relevant issues in the training of ITAs are discussed in Chapters Six and Seven.

How Should the Effectiveness of Training Be Evaluated?

The most obvious way to evaluate TA training programs is to look at the instructional work of the TAs who have participated in them. Any effort to prepare TAs to teach ought to be measured by TAs' effectiveness in the classroom. Some programs, such as the one at Syracuse University, are doing this sort of research-based assessment, but the number that do is small so far. There are good reasons why programs shy away from this sort of evaluation. Many programs are relatively new and still working to get activities, procedures, plans, and materials in place. Others are shoestring operations run by faculty and staff members who have many additional responsibilities and simply cannot take the time that this sort of evaluation requires.

Nevertheless, people associated with these programs do recognize the importance of evaluation and attempt in other ways to assess the effectiveness of training. Most commonly, this involves having participants complete some sort of survey at the conclusion of the activity. Several programs elaborate this initial evaluative information by conducting interviews with TAs several weeks after the program and well into the beginning of the semester. Still others regularly request feedback from departments about the propriety and relevance of training, from the departmental perspective. At the University of California at San Diego, an evaluation advisory committee, whose members are approved by the graduate school, coordinates assessment activities. The committee, looks at the participants' evaluations and conducts interviews. Few of these evaluation procedures could be considered rigorous, but they are typical of the kinds of effort used by most instructional and faculty development units to assess training activities, and they reflect the difficulty of evaluating such enormous yet elusive effects.

Conclusions

The foregoing discussion has attempted to summarize the wide-ranging TA training efforts in universities around the country. The institutions that cooperated by providing information about their programs represent small and large universities, public and private institutions. Most (but not all) have instructional/faculty development units, a trend that is becoming more prevalent at major institutions. In applying the lessons learned to an individual institution, the reader is advised to adapt, not adopt, since each institution is unique. By considering various options and selecting those most suited to the social and especially the political climate of your institution, you should be able to maximize benefits while minimizing resistance to TA training. You should also expect to continue tinkering with any training you devise, since no program in our sample did everything right the first time around.

Nevertheless, we can say with assurance that TA training can be done in ways that will meet almost any need at any institution with any resources at all. It is certainly the consensus of everyone involved in our survey that TA training is worth the effort—both to improve the quality of current teaching and to prepare future teachers.

Programs Surveyed and Persons Interviewed

Brown University
Center for the Advancement of College Teaching
Harriet Sheridan

University of California at Davis
Teaching Resources Center
Wini Anderson

University of California at Los Angeles
Teaching Assistant Training Program
(housed in Office of Instructional Development)
David Unruh

University of California at San Diego
Center for Teaching Development
John Andrews

University of Colorado
Graduate Teacher Program
Laura Border

Cornell University
Office of Instructional Support
David Taylor-Way

Harvard University
Danforth Center for Teaching and Learning
Eric Kristensen

University of Illinois
Division of Instructional Development
Marne Helgesen

University of Michigan at Ann Arbor
Center for Research on Learning and Teaching
Beverly Black

University of Missouri
TA Training and Development
Diane vom Saal

Ohio State University
Center for Teaching Excellence
Nancy Chism

Syracuse University
Teaching Assistant Program of the Graduate School
Leo Lambert

University of Washington
Center for Instructional Development and Research
Donald Wulff

University of Wyoming
Thomas Dunn

Maryellen Weimer is director of the Instructional Development Program, Pennsylvania State University.

Marilla D. Svinicki is associate director of the Center for Teaching Effectiveness, University of Texas, Austin.

Gabriele Bauer is a Ph.D. candidate, Pennsylvania State University.

Training programs for ITAs have multiplied in recent years but seem to fall into four types; appropriate staffing is the key to them all.

ITA Training Programs

Janet C. Constantinides

Only a few years ago, Fisher (1985) pointed out that the increasing number of international teaching assistants (ITAs) calls for more than a "quick 'language fix' " (p. 63). Although most current ITA training programs seem to acknowledge this fact, it still seems necessary to begin a discussion of ITA training program models by reiterating that point. Comprehensibility in English, although important, is not the only factor that determines the teaching success of ITAs. They also require orientation to the educational system of this country, as well as an understanding of the philosophy and the purpose of education that underlie the system. Since the behavioral expectations for students and teachers reflect the philosophy and purpose of an educational system, exploring the U.S. educational system should enable ITAs to understand the accepted and expected classroom behavior that ITA training programs should be designed to help them achieve. In addition, ITAs need awareness of and practice in the specific language skills necessary for successful classroom performance, whether as lecturers, discussion leaders, review session facilitators, lab instructors, or tutors. Because their previous experience as students in their home countries often has not introduced them to the roles they must play as teaching assistants, ITAs require not only training in such roles but time to make the transition from student in one culture to graduate student and teaching assistant in another.

This is not to say that comprehensibility is unimportant, but it is only the starting point. Successful ITA training programs have found that screening for oral language skills, beginning as early as the admissions process, is vital. Prospective ITAs who have not achieved adequate proficiency levels—for example, a score of 250 on the Test of Spoken English (TSE), which is a commonly used screening test—cannot benefit fully from a training program's emphasis on cross-cultural classroom communication skills or practice in teaching simulations. A language screening program alone, however, is not sufficient to assist ITAs with all the skills they need for teaching. Programs must also include ways of assisting ITAs with cross-cultural communication and teaching methods.

The purpose of this chapter is to discuss kinds of ITA training programs that include these emphases and to identify some of the ideas that should be considered for such programs to be successful.

ITA Training Programs

A review of the existing training programs for ITAs indicates that trainers generally use one of four approaches: orientation, presession programs, concurrent-term programs, or preterm programs.

Orientation. Orientations typically last from one to five days and are held just before the beginning of an academic term. Such programs focus on providing ITAs with information about the American postsecondary educational system, the institutions in which the ITAs will teach, specific requirements of departments, and the teaching assignments that ITAs will undertake. Trainers are often personnel from an institution's center for instructional development and from academic departments. If an orientation contains language emphasis, trainers from programs in English as a Second Language (ESL) may be involved. Some ITA orientations are part of larger orientation programs for new international students, and personnel from an international programs office or a foreign student adviser's office provide some of the instruction. Orientation programs typically include little if any specific work on English skills; because of the short time available, it is nearly impossible to change ITAs' use of English.

Orientation programs are relatively inexpensive, but they have limited effectiveness (Constantinides, 1987). The possibility of presenting too much information too quickly and the impossibility of effecting much change in language behavior in a short time are the greatest disadvantages of such programs.

Presession Programs. A presession program, lasting from one to four weeks before the start of an academic term, provides opportunities for addressing the cross-cultural, pedagogical, and language needs of ITAs. Such a program allows for training in cross-cultural communication skills, instructional methods, and language skills within the culture of the specific institution in which an ITA will teach. Individuals staffing the presession program may be from a center for instructional development, an ESL program, or academic departments in which ITAs teach. Faculty, especially, can provide information about expectations for TAs in specific departments.

One of the main advantages of this approach is that ITAs are able not only to receive information about the U.S. educational system, philosophy, and purpose but also to practice applying that information. Thus, they can change their teaching and language behavior before they begin teaching for the first time and perhaps avoid making the bad impression that often results when an ITA employs teaching behavior that may be considered exemplary in his or her home culture but may be confusing, if not offensive, to American students (for example, refusing to acknowledge students' questions). Wolocowitz (1982) discusses the important "implied contract" that is established the first day of class, which sets the tone for the rest of the term. If the ITA violates the expectations of American students or sets up conditions in an implied contract that are unacceptable or uncomfortable, it is very difficult to renegotiate the contract or overcome the bad impression established on the first day. The time available during presession training allows ITAs to begin to effect the changes in behavior, both pedagogical and linguistic, necessary to improve the classroom climate (vom Saal, 1987). Thus, trainers in a presession program must be thoroughly familiar with the culture of the institution and with the demographics and expectations of its students.

Concurrent-Term Programs. A concurrent-term training program occurs during the first term (ten to fifteen weeks) that the ITA teaches. This training program has several advantages. It provides more time for exploration of such issues as appropriate teaching behavior. It includes the chance to observe the teaching situations in which ITAs must function. It also enhances ITA's language skills. In this approach, faculty members from academic departments can provide specific information about the teaching tasks to be undertaken. Staff members from an instructional development center can also help ITAs develop appropriate teaching approaches. ESL instructors can provide instruction and practice in language skills, with special attention to the skills required by ITAs' teaching assignments (public speaking, discussion, responding to students' questions, giving instructions, acting as resource persons in labs, and so forth.

Programs that use this model report two major drawbacks. The first can be anticipated from the discussion of the "implied contract" (Wolocowitz, 1982). Often the ITA has already made a bad impression before there has been time in the training program to address the needed behavioral and language changes, and the ITA may not be able to recover from that situation before the end of the term. The second drawback is that the ITA may not be able to focus on the training because of the distractions of taking graduate courses and doing research. Since the ITA's main purpose is usually to succeed (indeed, to excel) as a student, he or she may relegate the work of the training program to last place, thus reducing the effect of the program.

Preterm Programs. A preterm training program represents the largest investment in time (and money) on the part of the institution in the training of ITAs. Such a program often lasts from ten to fifteen weeks and occurs during the term before the ITA interacts with undergraduates. It combines the advantages of the presession and concurrent-term programs by offering adequate time for the ITA to assimilate information about the U.S. educational system and about the specific institution and its students, as well as to practice the instructional skills and language need for success. A preterm training program does not put so much pressure on the ITA as the concurrent-term program, because a preterm program does not add the pressure of teaching to that of taking classes and doing research.

Staffing

The key to success in any of these approaches is the staff members who conduct the programs. If the focus of a training program is language, it is vital that ESL teachers know about the demographics of the institution's student population and be aware of the expectations for teachers' behavior. They must understand the varieties of teaching styles and methods accepted in different disciplines and tailor the language experiences of ITAs to prepare them to use appropriate language, both verbal and nonverbal (Constantinides and Byrd, 1986).

For the part of the program that emphasizes pedagogy, the staff members need knowledge of world educational systems, so that they can help ITAs undertake a contrasting study of their native systems and the U.S. system, with the goal of enabling ITAs to adapt to the different expectations of this system. When working with ITAs on communication skills, staff members need clear understanding, not just of general communication differences but also of special language and behavior required for success in teaching. Because personnel may operate from a perspective in which U.S. communication patterns are the norm, they must be cautious about using exercises and simulations that are inappropriate for ITAs from other cultures.

Faculty members from the academic departments who participate in training programs must clearly define the tasks that their ITAs will be assigned. These faculty members must also not assume that ITAs will have the same understanding of those tasks as their American counterparts do. For example, in some cultures, students do not have to wash glassware in the lab, because there are individuals specifically hired to do it. Thus, an ITA may not expect students to clean up the lab and may let them leave without doing so. Faculty members may also need orientation to differing education systems and cross-cultural communication skills, in order to understand the problems that ITAs may have in their teaching assignments.

In the ideal situation, of course, all training staff members are knowledgeable about all three areas and work as a team to design the program and help one another understand the important issues in each segment of it. The instructional development specialist should work with the academic departments to identify both the types of teaching tasks that ITAs will undertake and the preferred teaching methods of the various disciplines. That staff member can then collaborate with a cross-cultural communication specialist to identify differences in accepted communication performance between ITAs' native cultures and the United States, so that ITAs can meet the expectations of the institution's students. Similarly, an ESL specialist should tailor the language-specific part of the program to help ITAs learn the language skills demanded by successful communication.

Other Considerations

Other factors besides the program and staffing affect the success of ITA training. These include whether the training is compulsory, how ITAs' performance is evaluated, how ITAs' financial assistance is affected by the evaluations they receive, what follow-up is included, and what preparation undergraduates receive before having ITAs as teachers.

If an institution is committed to ensuring that every ITA who will teach is fully prepared to do so, then the program should be compulsory for any ITAs who cannot demonstrate that they are already fully prepared. Such an approach requires administrative enforcement. At the University of Wyoming, attendance from the first day of a three-week preterm program is a requirement for on assistantship award; failure to appear cancels the award.

If an ITA receives a grade in a training program, the grade should reflect the probability of his or her success in teaching. Because of their concern about grades, most ITAs prefer a pass-fail grade. At the University of Wyoming, a grade of "pass" indicates that the ITA can be expected to teach successfully. A grade of "conditional pass" indicates that the ITA may experience some difficulty and should be closely supervised. Ideally, faculty members from the academic departments should be involved in such evaluation decisions and should be included in the supervision process.

In such a graded system, another problem concerns what happens to an ITA who does not pass the training program and therefore cannot teach. If a university has included the ITA's assistantship money in certifying his or her eligibility for financial aid, then the school has an obligation to find some other way of funding the student. At the University of Wyoming, a department is required to continue the assistantship for one academic year, even if the ITA cannot teach. This practice protects students who do not pass the training course and simultaneously gives them another year to gain the necessary skills.

Follow-up should be a matter of concern to the entire training staff, not just to departmental faculty members or supervisors. Review of student evaluations, interviews with ITAs and their supervisors, and observations are some of the methods most often used.

One area that is still considered infrequently is the preparation of undergraduates who will be taught by ITAs. Vom Saal (1987) has described ways of attempting to orient American undergraduates to the cultural differences they may find in the classrooms of ITAs and of trying to change their attitudes toward having ITAs as instructors. Smith (1988) has produced a videotape to use with undergraduates and their parents in orientation programs. However, there is still much to be done in this area.

Conclusions

Training programs for ITAs have improved greatly in the last few years. Nevertheless, many institutions still have no programs, or only minimal programs. A training program that relies only on orientation may be better than nothing, but it is far from adequate to meet the complex needs of ITAs.

What makes their training even more important is that many of today's ITAs will be tomorrow's faculty members. This problem is not going to go away. Increases in the numbers of international students who are TAs precede increases in faculty members who are not native speakers of English and who have received at least part of their education in different cultures. In this sense, training ITAs is a form of faculty development for the future.

References

Constantinides, J. C. "Designing a Training Program for International Teaching Assistants." In N. Chism (ed.), *Employment and Education of Teaching Assistants: Readings from a National Conference.* Columbus: Center for Teaching Excellence, Ohio State University, 1987.
Constantinides, J. C., and Byrd, P. "Foreign TAs: What's the Big Problem?" *Journal of International Personnel,* 1986, *3,* 27–32.
Fisher, M. "Rethinking the 'Foreign TA Problem.'" In J.D.W. Andrews (ed.),

Strengthening the Teaching Assistant Faculty. New Directions for Teaching and Learning, no. 22. San Francisco: Jossey-Bass, 1985.

Smith, R. *You and the International TA: Paths to Better Understanding.* Washington, D.C.: National Association for Foreign Student Affairs, 1988.

vom Saal, D. R. "The Undergraduate Experience and International Teaching Assistants." In N. Chism (ed.), *Employment and Education of Teaching Assistants: Readings from a National Conference.* Columbus: Center for Teaching Excellence, Ohio State University, 1987.

Wolocowitz, J. "The First Day of Class." In M. M. Gullette (ed.), *The Art and Craft of Teaching.* Cambridge, Mass.: Harvard-Danforth Center for Teaching and Learning, 1982.

Janet C. Constantinides is assistant chair of the Department of English, University of Wyoming, and director of the Wyoming/NAFSA Institute on Foreign TA Training.

Many issues must be considered as ITA training programs evolve.

Issues in ITA Training Programs

Debra-L Sequeira, Magdalena Costantino

Those of us who work directly in international teaching assistant (ITA) training face two seemingly contradictory forces. On the one hand, undergraduates, their parents, legislators, faculty members, administrators, and trainers are concerned with improving the quality of undergraduate education. On the other hand, ITAs, who are often perceived as liabilities to the quality of undergraduate education, are needed on university campuses to effect an international exchange of ideas, assist in research programs, and perform important teaching roles. The tension that results from the meeting of these two forces raises a number of issues for all involved in undergraduate education, and particularly for those of us involved in training ITAs.

This chapter is designed to assist those who have been considering and reconsidering issues arising from the development of ITA programs. Our specific purpose is to identify significant issues in ITA training programs and suggest some future directions for addressing the questions they raise.

The ITA as Employee or Visiting Scholar

A major issue that ITA training programs must address right from the start is how the institution and its various constituencies view the role of the international teaching assistantship. Is it part of a job (in which ITAs are considered employees), part of an education (in which ITAs are considered visiting scholars), or some combination of both? There are several competing philosophical perspectives, and at many institutions these perspectives remain unclear or at least unstated.

One way of identifying the perspective of an institution is to listen to the language that people use when describing ITAs. The employee perspective views the ITA position as a means to an end, and often research is the end product. Any special training, according to this view, is part of the job, and any training should not take time away from graduate research. Thus, an ITA position puts bread on the table while the ITA focuses on research. The visiting-scholar perspective views the ITA position as one component of the graduate student experience. Teaching and research are seen as parts of an ongoing process in which teaching may even be required as part of a graduate program. Moreover, experienced TAs and faculty members are viewed as mentors. This viewpoint is applicable whether or not training the future professoriate is the goal. ITAs are learning a critical-thinking process from this culture, applying or adapting these skills when they return home. Thus, the ITA is a scholar in training during residency in the United States.

If ITA trainers understand the philosophical perspectives of their institutions, their ITA training programs can be grounded in these philosophies and increase the chances of institutional support for adequate training. For example, ITA trainers at research universities that maintain the employee perspective have successfully argued that effective training programs can save ITAs time for study and research. Institutions that emphasize teaching or some combination of teaching and research have focused on the potential of training programs to improve students' satisfaction and, ultimately, the quality of undergraduate education.

Screening for Proficiency in Oral English

A major policy issue in ITA training is how to assess oral proficiency in English. Because legislators, parents, and undergraduates who are concerned about ITAs as instructors have tended to focus on ITAs' oral English skills, there has been a trend toward legislation and development of policies for screening oral proficiency in English.

Today, most universities continue to admit and place international graduate students in programs on the basis of standardized screening tests, such as the Test of English as a Foreign Language (TOEFL), the Test of Spoken English (TSE), and the Speaking Proficiency English Assessment Kit (SPEAK). The advantage of standardized tests is that they provide comparative data for use in making decisions about the placement of ITAs. Because of concern about whether these tests measure a potential ITA's instructional readiness, however, they are no longer used as the only sources of preassessment data for the awarding of teaching assistantships.

Programs have increasingly incorporated interactive formats in the process of language assessment. Some programs use the standardized interview first developed in the Foreign Service Institute of the U.S. Department of State. (For a more detailed description of oral English proficiency tests and their advantages and disadvantages, see Plakans and Abraham, 1989.) Other programs have opted for interviews and performance testing of ITAs tailored to the needs of the institutions that will use them. For example, Southern Illinois University uses an oral interview as a screening method for potential ITAs. Michigan State University adds an instructional role-playing component to its interview format, in the form of an office-hour simulation. Pennsylvania State University uses an oral interview, coupled with a sample of the potential ITA's teaching, as part of the final screening for teacher certification after coursework in spoken English.

A number of institutions have incorporated variations of videotape critique as part of their assessment processes. For example, Georgia State University, Ohio State University, and the University of Wyoming require simulated teaching performances as a major component of screening and exit requirements in their ITA training programs. Iowa State University's videotaped simulation, the TEACH Test (Taped Evaluation of Assistant's Classroom Handling), has been supplementing the SPEAK since 1985. Many other colleges and universities include variations of microteaching as part of their ongoing training programs. As a form of assessment, microteaching with videotaping allows ITAs to see and hear how they look and sound while teaching.

Whatever the method or methods used, one thing is certain: Institutions are opting for more individualized pre- and post-competency requirements that assess instructional readiness. Confidence in these kinds of assessments, however, is a matter for concern, because with the emergence of less standardized measures come issues of establishing their degree of reliability and validity.

Course Training Versus Ongoing Training

One critical program issue is whether ITA training should be a course that ITAs must pass in order to teach or part of an ongoing program that assists ITAs throughout their employment. Many institutions provide ITA training courses. In some cases, ITAs must pass a course in order to be certified to interact with undergraduates. ITAs often receive funding until they are able to complete their ITA training coursework successfully. In some instances, these courses include a follow-up component, usually during and after the first term the ITA teaches. Proponents of the course approach to ITA training report that closure is important for ITAs and their departments. According to this view, once ITAs are certified to teach, their motivation increases, and students' complaints tend to decrease. (For a more complete discussion of the use of courses in ITA training, see Chapter Six.)

Institutions that adopt ongoing programs for their ITAs support training beyond an initial orientation or course, and beyond the first term that an ITA teaches. In such cases training uses a client-consultant model, in which the client is not in a course with other ITAs but is in a one-to-one relationship with a trainer or consultant. Individual consultations—based on videotape critiques, direct observations, students' feedback, and interviews with individual ITAs, departmental faculty members, and administrators—are the basis of the ongoing program. The program contains a follow-up component designed to assist ITAs by providing supervision, classroom observation, and instructional consultation for an academic year.

An ongoing program does require an investment in staffing and time, but proponents of this model cite a number of its advantages, particularly when it is combined with orientation sessions or workshops. Ongoing training addresses the complexity and variety of the situations that ITAs experience during their teaching. Because it is designed to account for the fact that ITAs may have differing instructional assignments in differing departments, where content and students may vary widely, the ongoing consulting model helps ITAs directly with the issues raised in their individual teaching situations. The ongoing training approach also allows sufficient time for ITAs to develop their skills, because it uses a systematic process that requires obtaining baseline information, setting goals for changes, implementing changes, assessing results, and establishing new goals—all at a time when ITAs have clearly defined instructional assignments in which to implement the training. Finally, the opportunity for individualization in the ongoing consulting model assists ITAs at a level appropriate to their individual development as international graduate students and instructors. (For a discussion of the developmental stages of TAs see Chapter Four.)

Although ITA trainers have become increasingly aware of the complexities of program-design issues, program development depends on the ways ITA positions are viewed and on the processes used for screening ITAs. Given the constraints of a particular institution and the needs of specific ITAs the training staff may find that courses, ongoing one-to-one consultations, or some combination may be most appropriate. Additional issues, such as staffing and curriculum, will also affect the final program design.

Staffing and Curriculum

Part of determining the responsibility for ITA training is to determine who will be responsible for such programs and who will staff them. Since one determinant of that responsibility is the curricular focus of the program, staffing and curriculum are interrelated.

Staffing. State legislatures and central administrative offices at institutions across the United States have largely been responsible for ITA training program requirements, but the units that conduct such training vary widely across campuses. Historically, such training has been housed in ESL programs. In some cases, however, other units on campus (such as instructional development centers or specific departments) have taken primary responsibility for ITA training. Because of the issues that arise when a single unit on campus houses the ITA training program, institutions must assess the comparative advantages of having only one unit responsible for training or having several involved.

A major concern is that a single unit cannot adequately address the diverse needs of ITAs. Some trainers have argued, for example, that ESL educators may not have questioned whether their own training approaches are adequate to prepare ITAs for instruction in specific academic disciplines (Byrd and Constantinides, 1988; Rounds, 1987). By contrast, others have maintained that instructional development centers, or specific departments without language specialists, cannot provide adequate language training for ITAs (see Chapter Six). A number of programs have responded to these concerns by including trained personnel in each of three content areas: ESL, instructional development, and cross-cultural communication. Many programs also enlist the expertise of other autonomous units on campus for an integration of training efforts.

Another issue related to staffing is the role that undergraduates can play in ITA training. At the University of Missouri at Columbia, undergraduates are involved in an interactive approach, in which they function as trainers as well as learners. They provide feedback during simulated teaching and receive information on intercultural skills designed to assist them in interacting with ITAs. Thus, these undergraduates have a direct impact on their own educational process, and they learn valuable intercultural communication strategies that will assist them "in preparation for their professional lives in an increasingly global marketplace" (vom Saal, 1987, p. 273).

Curriculum. Closely related to staffing is the issue of program emphasis. Although the issue for most undergraduates tends to be ITAs' "poor English," research suggests that ITAs also require extensive training in instruction and the kinds of cross-cultural communication appropriate for U.S. students (Swales and Rounds, 1985; Rounds, 1987). Training programs that equally emphasize three skill areas—language, pedagogy, and cross-cultural communication—maintain the perspective that "communicative competence" (Hymes, 1972) is the ultimate goal, because ITAs need to learn not only appropriate language but also appropriate behavior for specific contexts. To help ITAs achieve communicative competence in teaching in their disciplines, several programs are developing materials designed to address language needs in specific instructional contexts. The proponents of this training in English for specific purposes believe that ITAs need to develop language strategies specific to the instructional situations in which they interact with U.S. undergraduates.

Obviously, ITAs must have the language skills to master the instructional strategies most appropriate for teaching in their content areas. They also need information and instructional practice that will allow them to function cross-culturally in their particular universities. Institutions face the challenge of using experts in language, pedagogy, and cross-cultural communication (usually already present on most campuses) to address the complex needs of ITAs.

ITAs as Teachers of Minority Undergraduates

An increasingly critical issue of training prospective ITAs is preparing them for interaction with U.S. undergraduates. In the past, students were more homogeneous and were consequently taught as though they all learned in the same ways. Today, however, undergraduate populations are changing rapidly, and the kinds of generalizations originally presented to ITAs, to reduce their culture shock and information overload, are increasingly ineffective. Preparing ITAs for student diversity is particularly important in such departments as engineering, science, and management, the departments where many ITAs teach. Students who are typically considered "minority" elsewhere on campus often are the majority in these departments.

One way to help ITAs discover how to assist diverse undergraduate populations in their learning is to include diverse student groups in ITA training programs. The University of Washington's program, for example, includes minority undergraduates in workshops, so that ITAs can experience the diversity of perspectives the undergraduates bring to the classroom. Other approaches include interviewing the minority students taught by ITAs and talking with minority faculty members and multicultural educators to increase ITAs' awareness of current minority issues. (For additional strategies, see Chapter Three.)

Future Directions

The effort to achieve a balance between quality undergraduate education and the use of ITAs requires informed choices. To make informed choices, we need specific data. At one level, we can begin to obtain information about who is responsible for advising foreign students and minority students. We can locate the places where undergraduates go to complain about their TAs. We can identify the faculty members who coordinate orientation programs or TA training; and we can learn about faculty members' research on international or ethnic-minority education. On other levels, we need more substantive research. We still lack information on effective discipline-specific instruction (Byrd, 1986; Sequeira, 1986). ITA trainers must conduct research to discover the needs of undergraduate learners in disciplines where ITAs teach. Until we know what effective instructors do in each discipline, we will lack discipline-specific strategies to assist ITAs in instruction.

A way to begin is to discover who the effective instructors are in each discipline and ask them what they think works. ITA program staff members at the University of Michigan, Ohio State University, and the University of Washington, among others, have been conducting interviews and observations on campus, to discover effective teaching methods for various disciplines and develop strategies based on their discoveries. This discipline-specific approach to ITA training is more than "talking like a teacher," but talking like a mathematician, or an engineer, or a political scientist. There has been some advancement in the understanding of ITA issues in the teaching of mathematics, for example (Rounds, 1987), where we are now moving ITAs from the "talking book" approach to a more verbal elaboration in a step-by-step problem-solving process. Nevertheless, increased discipline-specific research would benefit all graduate assistants and faculty members, whatever their national origins. Just as there is a need for discipline-specific research, there is also a need for research on minority learners in specific disciplines. Once we discover what particular minorities think is effective for their learning, we can assist ITAs in the development of specific teaching strategies for their minority students.

Conclusions

If we intend to have successful training for ITAs, we must find ways to balance quality undergraduate education with the contributions that ITAs can make to it. We need to stop referring to the "foreign-TA problem." Instead, we must take a comprehensive approach, in which we continue to identify evolving issues, pursue multicultural research and training, and seek opportunities for communication exchanges among ITAs, faculty members, administrators, and undergraduates. By offering a comprehensive training program for ITAs, we increase the contribution they can make to the quality of undergraduate education. This is a benefit far too valuable to ignore.

References

Byrd, P. "Academic Subcultures Within U.S. Higher Education: Implications for FTA Training of Differences in Teaching Styles and Methods." *Papers of the Wyoming/NAFSA Institute on Foreign TA Training*, 1986, *1*, 2-10.

Byrd, P., and Constantinides, J. C. "FTA Training Programs: Searching for Appropriate Teaching Styles." *English for Specific Purposes*, 1988, 7 (2), 123-129.

Hymes, D. "On Communicative Competence." In J. B. Pride and J. Holmes (eds.), *Sociolinguistics*. New York: Penguin, 1972.

Plakans, B. S., and Abraham, R. G. "The Testing and Evaluation of ITAs." In D. Douglas (ed.), *English-Language Testing in U.S. Colleges and Universities*. Washington, D.C.: National Association for Foreign Student Affairs, 1989.

Rounds, P. L. "Characterizing Successful Classroom Discourse for NNS Teaching Assistant Training." *TESOL Quarterly*, 1987, *21* (4), 643-671.

Sequeira, D-L. "ITAs and the Road to Communication Competence: Learning to Map a Department." *Papers of the Wyoming/NAFSA Institute on Foreign TA Training*, 1986, *1*, 129-138.

Swales, J., and Rounds, P. L. *College Classroom Discourse*. Ann Arbor: University of Michigan, 1985.

vom Saal, D. R. "The Undergraduate Experience and International Teaching Assistants." In N. Chism (ed.), *Employment and Education of Teaching Assistants: Readings from a National Conference*. Columbus: Center for Teaching Excellence, Ohio State University, 1987.

Debra-L Sequeira is coordinator of the ITA Program at the Center for Instructional Development and Research, University of Washington.

Magdalena Costantino is an instructor at the Center for English as a Second Language in the Speech Communication Department, Pennsylvania State University.

Part 3.

New Directions in TA Training

Helping TAs use active learning strategies in their classrooms involves a wider range of issues than might be apparent at first.

Helping TAs Use Active Learning Strategies

Deborah H. Hatch, Christine R. Farris

Teachers have long realized that if they could get their students involved in the activities of learning, students would learn more and retain their new learning for a longer period of time. Activities that lead to such student involvement are commonly referred to as *active learning strategies*. Students' active learning strategies are produced by a wide range of teaching approaches, all aimed at helping students acquire new concepts, integrate these new concepts with old ones, and use this new structure of knowledge in critical thinking and problem solving. Teaching approaches based on facilitating active student involvement contrast dramatically with teaching approaches in which students passively receive, record, and eventually return the teacher's knowledge. Among the many teaching strategies that actively engage students are writing tasks, speaking activities, small-group activities, case-study methods of instruction, simulations, role plays, and field studies. In this chapter, we focus on training teaching assistants (TAs) to use active learning strategies based on writing and small-group discussion in the classroom.

In active learning situations, writing acts as a means to move students to higher levels of thinking, because it engages them in translating new ideas into their own words, in articulating relationships among ideas, and in integrating new information with prior knowledge to solve problems. Working collaboratively in groups also encourages higher levels of thinking by placing students in situations in which they encounter different approaches and perspectives and learn to accommodate conflict as well as to negotiate consensus.

Because of these benefits to undergraduate students, TA trainers and supervisors should help TAs learn to use active learning approaches. Helping TAs use active learning strategies in their classrooms involves a wider range of issues than might be apparent at first. It is not enough to suggest that TAs give their students writing tasks and divide students into small groups to work collaboratively. In designing and carrying out active learning strategies that will benefit their students, TAs must rely on their awareness of how they acquired their own knowledge and on their skill in translating this awareness into activities that help new learners acquire this knowledge. TAs must see themselves as master learners modeling thinking and learning for novice learners.

Unfortunately, this kind of awareness and skill is rare among new teachers; moreover, it is rarely reinforced by the situations in which most TAs find themselves. TAs often function primarily as convenient labor and merely interpret, review, test, and grade knowledge in a course. Such a passive model for teaching and learning has TAs working as somewhat disinterested advocates who help students figure out what the professor wants to see on quizzes, exams, and papers, even though the TAs will perform the bulk of the grading. With such passive, disengaged models for student-teacher interaction, it is unlikely that any of the excitement TAs feel about their own inquiry into their disciplines will find its way into their classrooms. It is also unlikely that TAs will come to include among their duties any responsibility for providing students the critical tools of the disciplines.

Given this situation, the task of TA trainers or supervisors is to figure out how to help TAs integrate active learning strategies into their classrooms. Although there are many ways of working with TAs (such as individual consultation, classroom observation, and videotape critiques), we focus on the workshop. In this chapter, we will discuss two workshops designed to help TAs use writing and small-group discussions as active learning strategies. Through these examples, we will illustrate these active learning strategies and examine the challenges TAs face in integrating these strategies into their classrooms. As the examples will illustrate, we have found that TAs are willing to consider and integrate active learning strategies into their classrooms, but only when we are willing to acknowledge the realities of passive models for teaching and learning under which they are working and to help them accommodate these realities.

Communication TAs: Seeing Themselves as Master Learners

In this example, we describe what occurred when a professor supervising a group of TAs who were teaching sections of a course in interpersonal communication consulted us to discuss the typical difficulties undergraduate students have writing required papers and to see if we could design a workshop that would help the TAs assist their students. The course introduces students to concepts and theories of interpersonal communication, and the paper assignments ask students to demonstrate their understanding by defining and illustrating these concepts and theories with analyses of examples from their own experience. From the TAs' perspective, the students were unable to perform either of these tasks successfully. Students' papers contained narrations of communication events but little or no analysis, and the TAs wondered why the students were unable to produce their papers from the information they were receiving in class and in their texts.

Our conversations with the TAs revealed that the paper assignments were consistent with the course goals and that students were receiving the necessary information to produce the papers, but our discussions also revealed that writing the papers was the only opportunity students had to engage in this task. Students submitted the papers in final form, without the opportunity to write drafts or receive critiques, and, perhaps more important, without spending time practicing the tasks required by the assignment. At first, the TAs were surprised by our interest in this point and asked if the papers were not themselves the practice. The TAs had not thought of the possibility of separating the tasks of the assignment and giving students practice with each task before asking them to write the papers, nor had they thought of asking students to write drafts. Was it possible that activities of this sort would make a difference in their students' performance? Our task was to convince the TAs that a sequence of short, ungraded writing assignments would be a good way of giving students the kind of practice that would help them to write their final papers, and that this process would actually enhance students' learning without creating more work for the TAs.

Since two of the major tasks of the papers were to demonstrate an understanding of a concept from interpersonal communication and to illustrate the concept through an analysis of a specific communication event, we worked with the TAs to design activities that would give students practice in each of these areas. When introducing a new concept in class, the TAs would give students five minutes to define the concept in their own words and then arrange students into small groups to compare their definitions and prepare group definitions to present to the rest of the class. In the next class meeting, TAs asked students to invent illustrations of the concept from their combined experience and present the illustrations to the class.

Such active learning strategies contrast significantly with the approach the TAs had been using before to introduce concepts and develop illustrations from them. Previously, TAs had presented the definition of a concept to the class, given a few specific illustrations of the concept from their own experience, and then called for volunteers from the class to give additional illustrations. Few volunteered, and their spur-of-the-moment illustrations were often superficial or inaccurate, shifting the responsibility back to the TAs to expand illustrations or clarify concepts through dialogue with individual students. Although other students could observe such dialogue, there was little to engage them.

The active learning strategies used in this course not only gave students important practice for their papers but also engaged all the students in the process of understanding concepts and developing and analyzing examples. By asking students to write definitions of a concept, the TAs were giving students time to collect and focus their thoughts. As one TA told us several days after trying this approach, "One of my students actually came up after class to thank me for giving him time to figure out what he thought. He said it really helped him get more out of the class." For most students, this time to write is very useful. For some, simply getting words on paper makes it easier for them to share these words with others. It is much less stressful for them to read what they have written than to speak unprepared. Writing has helped them rehearse their ideas. The examples generated in the small groups were also much more significant and developed than those elicited from volunteers. The groups also had more invested in their examples. Having students share what they have written in small groups is also helpful, since all the students are then engaged in discussions with one another. In small groups of three to five students, everyone has the opportunity to talk. In subsequent full-class discussions, small groups interact with one another, and the teacher's role becomes one of facilitating discussion among the groups.

What was most exciting in this example was the speed with which the TAs grasped these teaching possibilities and the enthusiasm with which they generated these and other activities. The TAs began to see their experience as learners as their true expertise. With this shift came a shift in emphasis, from written product to the process of writing. Abandoning their impatience with their students' inabilities to produce on the first try, TAs turned their attention to helping students discover the process of production. From this new perspective, TAs were able to use their experience as learners to help their students learn.

In this example, teaching TAs to use active learning strategies meant helping them uncover the source of their students' learning difficulties and then helping TAs see how they could aid learning by tapping their own expertise as learners. For TA trainers, there is an important lesson: without making this breakthrough in awareness, anything we would have said about active learning strategies might have fallen on deaf ears.

Art History TAs: Breaking Away from the Coverage Model

Although the shift to seeing themselves as learners can be relatively easy for TAs who are totally responsible for their courses, TAs who teach quiz sections in conjunction with large lecture courses, such as art history, face more challenges. For example, a course in which the professor lectures three hours a week to 450 students, and in which nine TAs meet two twenty-five-student quiz sections two hours a week, it is not surprising that the main issue for the majority of TAs is consistent coverage across the eighteen quiz sections. Moreover, the primary teaching goal is to keep up with other TAs, so that everyone's students will be equally prepared for the exams. For many TAs, this goal defines teachers as information providers, not model or master learners.

Despite working within such a course structure, several of the more experienced art history TAs had experimented with various techniques for expanding this role and wanted an opportunity to discuss their strategies with other TAs, as well as to gain new ideas. This group of TAs worked with us to plan a workshop in which they would describe some of their most successful strategies for stimulating discussion and then would answer questions raised by the other TAs and offer suggestions based on their experience.

Such a workshop design seemed well suited to the TAs' goals, but as the workshop began we realized that the TAs' perception of the need to cover content was much stronger than we had imagined. Uncertain of their responsibility to the professor, to their students, or to one another, the majority of the TAs concentrated on topic coverage, just to be safe, but even what constituted topic coverage provoked concern among the TAs. Was consistent coverage defined by the slides that the professor showed in the lectures, by the reproductions in the text, by slides that TAs showed in quiz sections, or by all three elements? A number of TAs reported showing everything that everyone else showed, just so that their students could not accuse them of leaving out something important. As one TA concluded, this strategy meant that his quiz sections consisted of one slide after another; there was certainly no time for discussion. For this TA, active learning strategies may be useful at some time in the future, when he is in control of the teaching situation, but not now.

Although these contextual realities had the potential to stop the workshop, they had the effect instead of directing TAs' attention to the purpose of the quiz sections and what the TAs would like to see happening there. They agreed that, ideally, a quiz section could be a place for students to practice, in a smaller setting, the methods of analysis they were observing in the lecture and reading in their texts. Questions of consistency and coverage could be redefined to refer not to rote information but to acquisition of concepts and analytical approaches. Students might not all see the same works of art, but all would practice the same methods of analysis.

Discussing this alternative class structure made such an option seem more attainable than it had before and made even the most coverage-burdened TAs receptive to their colleagues' descriptions of active learning strategies and to the suggestion of some TAs that they take the initiative to discuss these concerns with the professor. They listened with interest as a TA described an activity in which she divided the class into small groups, assigned each group one of the visual aspects of a work of art that art historians typically consider (light, color, line, space, movement, composition) and asked each small group to compare the handling of this element in the two slides projected on the screen. Each group kept track of its discussion through written notes and reported its conclusions, and each group's report was followed by a discussion of the different ways each artist handled the particular visual element. The TA concluded that this activity resulted in a productive discussion of visual elements, because each group of students was focused on a specific visual element and had time to think about it before joining in the full-class discussion.

Another TA described a short, writing-based activity that he used to begin a discussion of the analytical methods of art history. He asked students to turn in their lecture notes to the professor's analysis of two works and to take five minutes writing out the lecture's purpose and how the lecturer carried it out. Small groups of students then compared what they had written, reached consensus, and presented their conclusions. In the next quiz sections, this TA presented students with slides of two new works and asked them to analyze the slides by using what they had learned from their analysis of the professor's lecture.

In each of these descriptions, the TAs demonstrated the use of writing and small-group collaboration to help students learn. Their experience and enthusiasm convinced some of the other TAs to try to integrate these approaches into their quiz sections.

Our experience with these workshops reveals that TAs can be resistant to change because of the roles in which they find themselves. To help TAs consider active learning strategies, TA trainers have to acknowledge the perceived constraints under which TAs are working. Workshops such as these are hardly failures. Although they did not proceed according to the original plan, they accomplished a great deal.

Two Strategies to Promote Active Learning

Writing. In the art history example, the small groups of students focusing on different visual aspects of a work used writing to keep tract of their ideas and provide notes for their oral report to the rest of the class. The students writing about the lecturer's comparison of two works used writing to reflect on their lecture notes and discover patterns of analysis. Their writing was also the focus of their interaction with their peers as they compared and discussed one another's texts. The definitions that the communication students wrote of concepts in interpersonal communication helped them begin to assimilate abstract ideas. Like the art history students' lecture analyses, these written definitions provided a focus for small-group interactions. As the small groups of communication students worked together to develop illustrations of the concepts they had defined, writing recorded their ideas and gave them practice moving from generating ideas to composing.

Small-Group Discussion. In the art history quiz section, by dividing the class into small groups and assigning each group a single visual aspect to focus on, one TA accomplished a very efficient and effective division of labor. Each group became an authority on one aspect of the whole, and as each group reported, the overall analysis took shape for everyone. In subsequent class meetings, the TA could rotate the assignment of visual elements among the small groups so that, by the end of five or six such analyses, everyone would have had the opportunity to concentrate on all the visual elements. In addition to allowing a division of labor and a focus on specific tasks, small groups also allow the TA to show students the range of others' responses and interpretations that lectures, texts, and questions elicit, as well as strategies for accommodating differences and reaching consensus. The art history students who compared their analyses of the lecture's purpose in small groups quickly discovered that, although they had all heard the same lecture, they had all heard it slightly differently. The communication students comparing their definitions of concepts made a similar discovery. One value of asking small groups of students to compare their individual responses is that it introduces students to the range of responses that can occur with a particular boundary. Asking them to consider what their responses have in common and where they differ introduces them to the possibilities for consensus, as well as to an appreciation of genuine difference. It begins to wean them from the expectation of a "right" answer.

Responding to Resistance

By helping TAs use active learning strategies, we are promoting changes in how teachers teach and students learn. Since change of any kind often meets resistance, TA trainers must be aware of the resistance that TAs will meet, both from their students and from the faculty members for whom they work. This resistance may be expressed directly or indirectly; in either case, it must be acknowledged.

Students and professors alike may resist the use of active learning strategies. Students used to a passive model of instruction may resist a TA's attempts to engage them in active learning. Resistance can occur when students perceive inconsistency between the course goals expressed in the professor's lecture and the TA's goals in a quiz section. This resistance can be particularly strong if the students perceive that the method of evaluation used by the professor rewards the return of information, rather than the kind of critical thinking encouraged by active learning. Professors used to a model in which they hold complete responsibility for a course may be uncomfortable with the new role that active learning strategies assign to teachers, and they may discourage their TAs from adopting this role.

For TA trainers, these responses to active learning strategies raise the question of what to do when TAs who desire to use new teaching strategies are unable to gain the cooperation of students or of faculty members for whom they work. As TA trainers, we feel a responsibility to help TAs use the teaching strategies that are the most beneficial to their students, but our ability to help does not extend to the point of forcing students or faculty members to cooperate. Instead, we find ourselves working with TAs to find compromises that will benefit students. When students perceive that a TA's approach is inconsistent with the course professor's, it is important for the TA who wishes to use active learning strategies to help students see consistencies. When faculty members appear resistant to the teaching approaches TAs want to adopt, TAs need to learn how to share their perceptions of teaching and learning with them. TAs and faculty alike need to see that their students' learning is their common goal and need to work together to achieve it.

Conclusions

Our ability to help TAs use active learning strategies depends on our ability to work with the realities of TAs' situations. Designers of TA training programs should understand the roles that writing and small-group interaction can play in helping students learn and should be able to help TAs use these strategies in their classrooms. It is at least equally important to acknowledge the contextual realities that condition TAs' work and the effects of these realities on TAs' ability to use active learning strategies in their classrooms. If we do not acknowledge these realities, we are more likely to delay than to encourage the adoption of active learning strategies.

We admit that it can take years of working with students to really think of one's discipline as the best teachers do—not just from the scholar's point of view, but also from the novice's. Teachers who have been able to make this transformation as TAs, however, generally come to think of their relationship to both the students and the material in their courses more actively and interactively; their focus becomes more process-centered and less product-centered. Along with a growing confidence in their knowledge of the material, the effectiveness of their classroom strategies, and their ability to affect students' learning comes a belief that, as teachers, they can make a difference. Their students may become actively engaged in learning, to the point of not only performing well in a course but perhaps also choosing the discipline as a major and a career. That level of student-teacher interaction empowers everyone: Students have something invested in their learning and choose to remain in the academy, and TAs experience less of the alienation that is too often said to go with the territory. They join the professoriate as effective teachers, as well as scholars, and academic disciplines remain stimulating sites of inquiry for everyone, not just for the elite.

Deborah H. Hatch is a lecturer in the University of Washington's Interdisciplinary Writing Program and a writing consultant at the University of Washington's Center for Instructional Development and Research.

Christine R. Farris is assistant professor of English at the University of Missouri.

By focusing attention on assessing, understanding, and improving learning, classroom research can empower teaching assistants and their students to improve the effectiveness of higher education.

Classroom Research for Teaching Assistants

Thomas A. Angelo, K. Patricia Cross

In the 1990s, higher education will face two challenges with respect to the future professoriate, one quantitative and the other qualitative. First, to meet the staffing needs of the nation's colleges and universities, we must encourage more of our best graduate students to choose college teaching as a career. Second, to maintain and improve the quality of higher education, we must prepare these future faculty members to teach more effectively and to value teaching as a profession that requires mastery of skills, as well as knowledge of subject matter.

During the coming decade, because of the confluence of powerful demographic, economic, and educational trends, this dual challenge will offer an unprecedented opportunity to improve the quality of higher education in the U.S. Those of us concerned with preparing graduate teaching assistants (TAs) for college teaching can make the best use of this "window of opportunity" by focusing our collective energies on a common goal: preparing TAs for their probable futures as college teachers.

The Challenge of Quantity

After the much-publicized "glut" of Ph.D.'s in the 1970s and 1980s, a period during which many people with new doctorates failed to find permanent academic appointments, the nation faces a likely shortfall of candidates for faculty positions in the 1990s and beyond. What has long been a buyer's market is swiftly becoming a seller's market.

Projections indicate that about half of those currently teaching in colleges will reach retirement age in the next ten to fifteen years. During the same period, the number of young people entering college will swell appreciably, as the children of the post–World War II generation come of age. As a result, in the coming decade, America's graduate schools will have to educate and train thousands of graduate students to replace the waves of retiring faculty.

It will not be enough to prepare and hire vast numbers of new college teachers, as difficult as that task is in itself. We must build a more diverse national faculty as well. There is virtually unanimous agreement among educational leaders that the professoriate of the twenty-first century must include a much greater proportion of women and members of currently underrepresented minority groups.

The predicted shortfall in quantity of college faculty members is usually blamed on forces beyond academic control, such as economic and demographic trends. While higher education is expected to respond to these trends, few hold the academic community responsible for the problem itself. In contrast, most observers argue that the perceived shortfall in the quality of college teaching faculty is basically a result of choices made within higher education.

The Challenge of Quality

Since the mid 1980s, growing public concern over the quality of higher education has been expressed in the rhetoric of reform reports and in the reality of legislative mandates for higher standards and greater accountability. Fears that the United States is losing ground in an increasingly competitive global economy have made educational quality a major public policy issue. At the same time, rapidly rising costs and greater competition for available funds are forcing colleges and universities to assess and document the quality of learning outcomes for skeptical state legislators, governors, taxpayers, and parents, who demand to know what kinds of return they are getting on their investments.

In the last few years, there have been many calls for change in the training of college teachers. For example, the Association of American Colleges insists that teaching must come first for faculty in undergraduate programs, and that this message must be "forcefully delivered by academic leaders responsible for undergraduate education to the research universities that have awarded the Ph.D. degree to generation after generation of professors professionally unprepared to teach" (Association of American Colleges, 1985, p. 11). Lest we think lack of preparation is a new problem, however, these words from a report on a 1949 meeting of the American Council on Education suggest that little has changed in forty years: "The American college teacher is the only high-level professional man in the American scene who enters upon a career with neither the prerequisite trial of competence nor experience in the use of the tools of his profession" (Blegen and Cooper, 1950, p. 123).

Prodded into action by critical reports and local pressure, college presidents, deans, faculty developers, and faculty members are taking a hard look at their institutions' programs for preparing graduate students to teach and are too often finding them inadequate, or nonexistent. One concern is the immediate quality of instruction provided to the institutions' own undergraduates by ill-prepared TAs. A second concern lies in the preparation of today's graduate students as tomorrow's faculty members. The conviction is growing that the TA experience should become a valuable "apprenticeship to a lifelong career" rather than just "a convenient way for the university to disburse financial aid" (Boehrer and Sarkisian, 1985, p. 7).

The purpose of this chapter is to explore the potential contribution of classroom research as a tool in the training of TAs. By collecting data on what students are learning in their classrooms, teachers can assess the effectiveness of their own teaching. This self-assessment is particularly important for new and beginning teachers.

The Nature of Classroom Research

Classroom research is a term we use to describe a learner-centered, teacher-directed approach to improving the effectiveness of higher education where it matters most—in the college classroom. The primary purpose of classroom research is to improve the quality of learning in college classrooms by improving the effectiveness of teaching. Training in classroom research methods and techniques helps individual college teachers obtain useful feedback on what, how much, and how well their students are learning. Teachers then use that information to refocus their teaching to improve learning. As teachers practice classroom research, they become better able to understand and promote learning and increase their ability to help students become more effective, self-directed learners. In brief, the main goal of classroom research is to empower teachers and their students to improve the quality of college learning.

In 1988, with support from the Pew Charitable Trusts and the Ford Foundation, we launched the University of California at Berkeley Classroom Research Project. Its purpose is to develop methods and materials needed to encourage and train college teachers to become classroom researchers, effective assessors of the learning of students in their classrooms. The U.C. Berkeley Classroom Research Project has roots in three widespread approaches to improving higher education: the assessment movement, educational research, and faculty development. In each case, however, the Classroom Research Project seeks to bring the benefits of these approaches into the college classroom and under the direction of the individual teacher.

First, it brings assessment, usually practiced at the system or campus level, directly into classrooms, where the mission of colleges is carried out. Second, classroom research seeks to reduce the gap between educational research and teaching practice to zero, by providing teachers with the tools needed to conduct action-oriented, applied research in their own classrooms. Third, classroom research extends faculty development by encouraging teachers not only to apply innovative teaching techniques but also to systematically assess the effects of those innovations on student learning.

While all good teachers gather information on their students' learning, very few do so systematically and regularly enough to use that feedback to improve the quality of learning. Much of the information that college teachers do collect is used to sort and grade students at the end of units or courses. Even if grading and sorting students are not pleasant tasks for many, most teachers become fairly adept at summative assessment through practice.

Most college teachers are not so adept, however, at formative assessment, at getting information early and regularly enough to avoid or defuse learning problems and keep learners on track. For example, most experienced teachers monitor and react to students' questions, comments made during class discussions, body language, and facial expressions in an almost automatic fashion as they are teaching. This automatization of eliciting and responding to students' feedback is a skill that normally takes TAs several years to develop.

The greater part of the feedback that experienced teachers depend on to make ongoing assessments of students' learning and lightning-fast adjustments in their teaching is diffuse and quickly lost. Since these interactions are so complex and happen so quickly, few teachers can recall much about them after a session is over. Much of the classroom information that could inform teaching is not used, simply because it is not systematically collected or analyzed.

In sum, most experienced college teachers develop appropriate ways to determine how well and how much students have learned by the end of a semester. They are much less skilled, however, at evaluating students' learning during the semester, or at gaining insights into "sticking points" along the way. While TAs have to learn both skills, they begin with a head start in summative assessment, having had many years to learn from examples (both good and bad) of how to give quizzes, tests, and exams. Explicit formative assessment, by contrast, is a skill that veteran and novice teachers need help to develop. Classroom research is designed specifically to develop that skill.

The Process of Classroom Research

One of the purposes of classroom research is to help teachers develop simple ways to investigate, document, and analyze students' learning in progress. To do this, teachers have to learn to focus and control the amount and type of feedback they elicit on their students' learning. The U.C. Berkeley Classroom Research Project offers college faculty a step-by-step procedure for learning to carry out simple classroom research projects.

Classroom Assessment. We refer to first-stage classroom research projects as *classroom assessment*. These projects are designed to evaluate the accomplishment of a single important course goal, such as the improvement of writing or problem-solving skills. In the U.C. Berkeley Classroom Research Project, initial training in classroom assessment takes place in a workshop of eight to ten hours, usually held over a day and a half. In the introductory workshop session, participants use a specially designed goals survey, the Teaching Goals Inventory, to identify and rate the relative importance of their course goals. This exercise encourages each participating teacher to focus on assessing one important teaching or learning goal in one course. No attempt is made to guide the teacher's choice of a goal to assess. Up to this point, however, many more teachers have focused on skill- or process-related goals than on goals concerned with specific course content.

Once the faculty member has selected a particular course and rated teaching goals, he or she considers the kinds of feedback that could be collected on learning related to the goals and identifies assessment techniques for getting that information. Many participants begin by adapting one of the simple assessment techniques described in *Classroom Assessment Techniques: A Handbook for Faculty* (Cross and Angelo, 1988). Faculty members are encouraged, however, to design and field-test assessment techniques of their own devising, techniques specially tailored to their disciplines, curricula, and students. After modeling their first assessment techniques on those in the *Handbook,* several teachers have gone on to create their own ingenious feedback devices.

Although teachers are free to carry out their projects independently, almost none choose to do so. Over and over, the participants report that discussing teaching and learning problems with their colleagues, particularly those from their own departments, is one of the most valuable outcomes of the project. The most effective working arrangement to date involves pairs and small teams of teachers from the same or like disciplines getting together as needed to discuss and assist each other throughout their projects. After most participants on a given campus have completed a classroom assessment project cycle, the whole group convenes for reporting. At this stage, faculty members from various disciplines are ready and eager to learn from one another and are able to draw useful analogies among projects and problems in different fields.

Classroom Research. More than one hundred teachers from four community colleges and two private four-year colleges have been involved in the project to date. In general, they are eager to take on bigger issues than a single classroom assessment project can address. Therefore, once participants feel comfortable with classroom assessment, they are encouraged to design more complex, longer-term projects. These more ambitious projects, some of which continue for a year or more, often incorporate classroom assessment techniques but always go beyond them. In this way, classroom research is more than the sum of discrete classroom assessment projects; it is the continuous, ongoing, developing study of teaching and learning in the classroom through a wide variety of appropriate means selected and controlled by the teachers themselves.

Classroom assessment is the most clearly elaborated element of classroom research to date, but many other ways to study students' learning in the classroom need to be explored. For example, classroom researchers could mine the rich information on critical and creative thinking that is buried in classroom tests and homework assignments, term papers, and problem sets. They could develop more effective ways to use short, focused interviews and surveys to assess the effects of course activities on beliefs, values, and dispositions. To fulfill its promise, classroom research must become a vehicle for understanding and improving the entire range of learning goals that college teachers have for their students and that students have for themselves.

Characteristics of TA Training Programs

On the basis of our observations and experiences, we have categorized TA training programs into four general approaches. These four categories, named for the characteristic types of services offered to TAs in each approach, are the inspiration/information approach, specific skills training, clinical/technical consultation, and coaching/mentorship. These approaches to preservice TA training parallel and are sometimes the same as those used for inservice faculty development. Most faculty development and TA training programs make use of more than one of these approaches.

Table 1 presents some of the defining characteristics of the four approaches to TA training. The inspiration/information approach relies mostly on speeches and lecture demonstrations by teaching experts, who may be TA trainers, local faculty members recognized for their excellent

Table 1. Characteristics of Four Common Approaches to TA Development

Approach	Commonly Used Techniques	Characteristic Role of TA Developer or Faculty Member	Characteristic Role of Participating TA
Information/ inspiration	Speeches, lectures, teaching demonstrations	Organizer/ speaker/presenter	Audience
Specific skills training	Workshops and seminars	Organizer/trainer	Trainee
Clinical/ technical consultation	Observation, videotaping, one-to-one consulting	Consultant/ therapist/adviser	Client or advisee
Coaching/ mentorship	Observation, informal and structured observations	Coach/mentor	Apprentice

teaching, or nationally known authorities on college teaching. The aims of this approach are to inform TAs how to teach effectively and inspire them to work toward that goal. These presentations are often one-shot, stand-alone affairs, though they can be effectively integrated into ongoing TA training programs. The participation of TAs in these sessions is usually rather passive, limited to listening to and asking questions of speakers.

Programs designed to provide specific skills training require TAs to participate more actively as trainees. The purpose of such programs is to develop skills and techniques that will help TAs teach more effectively. Training workshops, seminars, and short institutes focus on questioning techniques, skills needed to lead discussions, grading practices, and the like. Although TAs may be surveyed about the areas in which they would like training, the agenda for a skills workshop is set primarily to meet the needs of the group, and only secondarily those of the individual teacher.

The heart of clinical/technical consultation is the one-to-one conversations that take place between the TA and the teaching consultant. The TA developer plays a highly personal role as therapist, adviser, or problem fixer, while the TA is the client or advisee. Such consultation can focus on improving teaching techniques, on the one hand, or on the deeper personal issues of the TA's feelings and reflections about teaching, on the other. In contrast to the two previously mentioned approaches, TA clients usually set the agenda for the consultation. In some programs, all TAs participate in consultations; in others, the services are available but voluntary. In a third type of program (probably the most problematic), TAs are referred for consultation by faculty members or TA trainers only if the TAs are perceived as having difficulties in the classroom.

The fourth approach, coaching/mentorship, shares with the consultative model the advantages of one-to-one personal contact, but in this case the helping other is a faculty member, usually from the same discipline and often an experienced and well-regarded teacher. In practice, the differences between coaching and mentorship consist largely in degree of time commitment and depth of relationship between TA and faculty member. In both cases, the TA serves a kind of apprenticeship, learning by watching, working with, and talking with the master teacher. The purpose of such arranged partnerships is for veterans to pass on the craft of teaching by sharing their wisdom and experience with novices. Katz and Henry (1988) provided an excellent guide to mentoring for faculty development.

Classroom Research for TA Training

Classroom research, in this application, explicitly draws on each of the other four approaches. In classroom research projects, the workshop leader provides inspiration and information, as well as specific training in teaching and assessment skills. While technical and even clinical consultation may be provided by the TA developer, participating TAs and faculty members play important roles as coconsultants during the projects. Peer coaching and support are central to most classroom research projects, and there are many opportunities for informal or formal mentoring.

There are two important differences, however, between classroom research and the other four approaches to TA development. The first difference is focus. The primary purpose of classroom research is to improve students' learning. Its intention is to focus attention on students' progress and achievement as indicators of how well teachers are teaching. The second difference is one of degree. Classroom research requires participants to show a greater degree of initiative and self-direction than the other approaches do. For classroom research to succeed, participants must assume responsibility for their individual projects by raising questions about their teaching, devising projects to explore those questions, and collecting and interpreting data on student learning.

TA developers have a critical role to play by stimulating interest in classroom research, organizing projects, providing initial training, and offering ongoing support to individual and group efforts. At the same time, TA developers must refrain from explicitly or implicitly setting the agenda. After the initial training workshop, the TA developer in a classroom research program is primarily a facilitator and secondarily a resource.

While TAs and veteran faculty members share many concerns about students' learning, TAs will need more systematic support from TA trainers to make classroom research an integral part of their teaching practice. Because of their limited teaching experience, for example, TAs need more help framing researchable questions about students' learning and more time to formulate and carry out projects, and they may find it difficult to manage assessment and teaching at the same time.

Perhaps the most effective way for TAs to learn to use classroom research techniques is to work in pairs or small teams with other TAs and experienced faculty members from their disciplines. Supervising teachers can organize team projects for all the TAs teaching sections of a specific course or within a given department. Focusing attention on assessing students' learning of one important, commonly held teaching goal can be very informative. Once TAs develop classroom assessment skills and self-confidence through carrying out simple pair or team projects, they can be encouraged to pursue more ambitious, personally relevant questions.

Classroom research is potentially a powerful way to help TAs learn important practical lessons about their students' learning, their own teaching, and, more generally, about teaching and learning in their disciplines. Through the ongoing practice of classroom research, TAs can develop both the skills and the knowledge they need for becoming effective, learner-centered teachers.

References

Association of American Colleges. *Integrity in the College Curriculum: A Report to the Academic Community.* Washington, D.C.: Association of American Colleges, 1985.

Blegen, T. C., and Cooper, R. M. (eds). *The Preparation of Teachers.* Washington, D.C.: American Council on Education, 1950.

Boehrer, J., and Sarkisian, E. "The Teaching Assistant's Point of View." In J.D.W. Andrews (ed.), *Strengthening the Teaching Assistant Faculty.* New Directions for Teaching and Learning, no. 22. San Francisco: Jossey-Bass, 1985.

Cross, K. P., and Angelo, T. A. *Classroom Assessment Techniques: A Handbook for Faculty.* Ann Arbor, Mich: National Center for Research to Improve Postsecondary Teaching and Learning, 1988.

Katz, J., and Henry, M. *Turning Professors into Teachers: A New Approach to Faculty Development and Student Learning.* New York: Macmillan, 1988.

Thomas A. Angelo is a lecturer in higher education in the Graduate School of Education, University of California at Berkeley, and assistant director of the U.C. Berkeley Classroom Research Project.

K. Patricia Cross is Conner Professor of Higher Education, Graduate School of Education, University of California at Berkeley, and director of the U.C. Berkeley Classroom Research Project.

Part 4.

Research and Resources for TA Training

More research on training strategies is needed to inform the practices of TA training.

Review of Research on TA Training

Robert D. Abbott, Donald H. Wulff, C. Kati Szego

One way to enhance the training of teaching assistants (TAs) is to ground practice in the research investigating the effects of various kinds of training. To understand more fully what the research on TA training might contribute to actual practice and further inquiry, we examined research on TA training. We began with the work of Carroll (1980) and Levinson-Rose and Menges (1981), who present comprehensive appraisals of the research on TA and faculty training methods before 1980. As we examined these two reviews, we discovered that research was scant prior to 1980 on the efficacy of different approaches to TA training. In fact, in his analysis, Carroll (1980) called for "substantially more effort . . . devoted to assessing the effects of TA training programs rather than simply describing innovative ways of conducting such programs" (p. 176).

To examine the extent to which TA trainers and researchers have responded to Carroll's call, we identified the research on TAs since 1980. The goals of this chapter are to review this research, comparing the effectiveness of components of TA training programs; to examine the research on TAs' characteristics as they are related to student ratings and achievement; and to discuss our conclusions and future directions for research.

Procedures

We employed three strategies to identify research relevant to the training of TAs. Because we assumed that research since 1980 that has focused on TA training would cite the comprehensive reviews of Carroll (1980) and Levinson-Rose and Menges (1981), our first strategy was to identify all the articles that referred to these two reviews. Second, we conducted a search in ERIC, from 1980 to December 1988. We selected journal articles and conference papers from among 304 ERIC bibliographical references to TAs. Third, to identify research that might have escaped the ERIC reference list, we systematically surveyed national journals that published research on higher education from 1980 to the present, as well as selected journals in instructional development. Added to this list were twenty-three discipline-specific educational journals. We used the broadest of criteria for initial selection of articles: any research with evidence of systematic evaluation of TAs' performance, needs, and so forth, or descriptions of TA training efforts. We identified (but excluded from further consideration) general descriptions of TA training programs, general descriptions accompanied by immediate participant-satisfaction measures, results from national surveys on TAs' needs, and articles on undergraduates functioning as peer tutors or proctors. Because these sources did not include systematic comparisons with data on untrained TAs, we did not include them in this review.

As we collected and reviewed articles, distinct categories emerged. We made preliminary assignments of articles to nine different categories and established the following classification of sources for final inclusion: (1) reports on components of TA training programs, (2) research on TA characteristics correlated with student ratings or achievement, and (3) articles that reported relationships among self, supervisor's, and/or students' ratings of TAs.

Research on Components of Training Programs

The articles discussed in this section investigated the effects of TA training methods and used a research design that manipulated variables with training (TG) and no-training groups (NTG) or employed pre- and posttesting. Of the thirteen studies identified, all reported significant effects on the basis of some aspects of the training provided for TAs. As the description of the studies in Table 1 indicates, there was some variation in the elements of training that were researched, the extent of the effects, and the ways in which effects were measured.

Student Ratings with Consultation or Interpretation. We identified four studies that examined the effects on TAs of student ratings combined with consultation or interpretation. McKeachie and others (1980) randomly assigned TAs to one of three groups: personal feedback of student ratings, with consultation from an experienced teacher; computer printout of ratings only; and no ratings. Their results support the primary hypothesis that instructors who receive consultation about their ratings are rated most effective at the end of the term. A study by Bingman (1983) used two groups. One received summaries of student evaluations from the previous quarter, interpretations of evaluation results, and follow-up assistance, including a training seminar. The other received student evaluations but no follow-up or additional training services. Like McKeachie, Bingman found significantly higher ratings for the treatment group. The importance of specific behavioral feedback from student ratings is also supported in a recent study by Murray and Smith (1989), who found dramatic changes in TAs' behavior when TAs were given specific midterm ratings feedback with instructions for interpretation, as compared to a control group that received no ratings feedback. In contrast to these three studies, Bray and Howard (1980) found that consultation based on student ratings was not sufficient by itself to produce changes in end-of-course ratings.

The studies cited here suggest that consultation based on student ratings can be useful in helping TAs improve their teaching. TA programs that include standardized ratings and other forms of feedback about students' perceptions, however, may need to address how consultation can be incorporated effectively into the TA training process.

General Training Combined with Videotaping. Of the studies identified, three found positive effects for general training programs that included some variation of videotaping combined with self-evaluation or consultation with an expert. In a study conducted with pharmacy graduate students who taught undergraduates, Hendricson and others (1983) focused on the use of videotaping and classroom observation. Using pre- and postratings of videotaped lectures, the researchers concluded that providing TAs with feedback on their videotaped lecture performance, as well as critiques from trained classroom observers, improved the quality of subsequent lectures. In another study that incorporated videotaping, Dalgaard (1982) compared treatment and control groups of TAs when the training consisted of six two-hour seminars, self-evaluation, and goal-setting based on both pretraining and posttraining videotapes. When the two groups were compared on the basis of planning instruction to meet clear goals, organizing content in a logical fashion, and involving students in instruction, trained TAs received significantly higher ratings. In their efforts to study the videotape training component, Bray and Howard (1980) found that a training seminar and videotape feedback with consultation were effective in producing change. In this study, however, the contribution of the training seminar was not clear, since the ratings for the group that received seminar and videotape consultation were not significantly different from those for the group that received consultation focused only on videotaped feedback.

Table 1. Research on Components of Training Programs

Reference	TAs/Disciplines	Training and Research Format	Measures	Results
Andrews (1981)	4 TAs Chemistry	**TG:** peer-centered and instructor-centered styles	Pretest students' learning styles; posttest students' ratings of teaching styles; course grades	Learning improves with TAs' socioemotional sensitivity and empathy
Bingman (1983)	12 TAs Varied departments	**TG:** student-ratings consultation; seminars on lecturing, testing, questioning, etc. **NTG**	Pre/post student ratings	**TG** received higher ratings than **NTG** on all items[a]
Bray and Howard (1980)	38 TAs Varied departments	**TG1:** seminar, video, and student-ratings consultation **TG2:** video consultation **TG3:** student-ratings consultation **NTG**	Pre/post student ratings, self-ratings, video	**TG**s produced positive changes in teaching behavior, self-ratings, and student ratings relative to **NTG**
Dalgaard (1982)	22 TAs Economics, geography, business administration	**TG:** seminars, video consultation **NTG**	Pre/post video	**TG** received higher overall rating of teaching than **NTG**[a]
Garner and others (1987)	ca. 50 TAs Foreign languages	**TG:** faculty demos, model video, microteaching, etc.	Pre/posttest of foreign-language methods	All TAs improved (no test of statistical significance)
Hendricson and others (1983)	7 residents Pharmacy	**TG:** consultation on video and classroom observations	Pre/post video	**TG** improved lecturing skills[a]

Study	Sample	Treatment	Measures	Results
Johnson (1987)	15 TAs Varied departments	**TG:** Cognitive Interaction Analysis System	Pre/post audiotape	**TG** changed verbal behavior, increased interaction with students[a]
Kanaga (1979)	26 TAs Speech communication	**TG:** small-group processes; **NTG**	Mid/posttraining student ratings	**TG** produced more appropriate levels of teaching performance than **NTG**[a]
Liggett (1986)	12 TAs English	**TG:** grading seminars	Pre/post grading procedures	**TG** acquired modeled procedures (no test of statistical significance)
McKeachie and others (1980)	37 TAs Psychology	**TG1:** student-ratings consultation **TG2:** student ratings only **NTG**	Pre/post student ratings; student achievement	**TG1** improved most[a]
Murray and Smith (1989)	60 TAs Psychology, English, geography	**TG:** specific behavioral feedback through student ratings **NTG**	Pre/post student ratings	**TG** received higher mean ratings for teaching improvement
Rodriguez (1985)	28 TAs Varied departments	**TG:** reinforcement, summary, questioning techniques, lecture and video critiques **NTG**	Posttest classroom observation	**TG** produced short-term changes in verbal behavior[a]
Sharp (1981)	37 TAs Varied departments	**TG1:** training and viewing of model video **TG2:** training only	Pre/post microteaching; TAs' interest and relevance ratings of model video topic	**TG** produced modeled behavior; interest in modeled topic does not predict performance

Note: **TG** = training group; **NTG** = no training group.
[a] Significant difference

We identified three other studies that included some variation of videotaping with peer feedback. In a study by Rodriguez (1985), training consisted of a one-hour conference and a three-hour training session focused on helping TAs use reinforcement, summary, and question-asking procedures. As part of the program, TAs prepared and presented fifteen-minute lectures using the techniques learned, received feedback from other TAs, and evaluated their videotaped performance. Rodriguez concludes that feedback and the videotapes were effective for providing practice and allowing TAs to recognize and adopt reinforcement, summary, and questioning procedures. Garner and others (1987) developed a five-day interdepartmental training program that included videotaping in the form of microteaching. The training, which was conducted with five foreign-language departments, focused on issues in teaching languages and included demonstrations by faculty members and experienced TAs, as well as cross-language microteaching. The researchers concluded that through the workshop TAs increased their knowledge of methods and techniques for teaching foreign languages. In addition, TAs cited the microteaching as the most useful activity of the workshop. Sharp (1981) also used microteaching as part of an orientation workshop, but primarily as a pre- and posttest measure to determine the effects of a model videotape. In this study, all trainees participated in an initial microteaching session, a lecture skills workshop, and a second microteaching workshop. The treatment group also viewed a model videotape on effective lecturing. In addition, Sharp assessed the TAs' interest in the topic modeled in the videotape and the TAs' perceptions of the relevance of that topic, to determine possible effects on TAs' acquisition of the modeled behaviors. Results of this study indicate that the videotape did produce a significant effect on the acquisition of modeled behaviors by TAs, as assessed by trained observers. Sharp further concludes that trainees need not perceive the modeled topic as interesting or relevant in order for a model videotape to be effective.

The studies that focused on videotaping as part of a training program suggest that videotaping, with self- or consultant-analysis and goal setting, can be effective in producing change in TAs. Studies that used variations of videotaping suggest that peer feedback, microteaching, and model videotapes are all uses of videotape that can be incorporated successfully into TA training programs. Trainers who use videotaping in their programs, however, may want to consider how such videotaping can be incorporated in ways that balance the outcomes with the constraints of time and resources.

Training in Specific Disciplines. We located two studies focusing on discipline-specific training for TAs. In attempting to improve the grading practices of TAs teaching freshman composition, Liggett (1986), used a pre- and posttest design to assess the effects of a semester-long training program that consisted of three hours of meetings per week. Training included readings about evaluation, six paper-grading sessions focused on comparison of comments and grades on student essays, and a mentoring program in which new TAs were paired with veteran TAs who checked sets of marked essays for validity and reliability of comments and grades. Liggett concludes that the training sessions influenced how new TAs marked papers. Furthermore, the influences were perceived as positive, on the basis of comments from teachers, students, and mentors. Kanaga (1979) examined the effects of a training program designed to prepare undergraduate TAs as section leaders in speech communication courses. TAs in a training group participated in four three-hour training sessions designed to increase confidence in their leadership skills, to demonstrate the use of various class exercises, and provide practice in applying their skills in situations where constructive feedback was provided. Kanaga concludes that the training was somewhat successful. When compared to a control group with no training, the trained TAs were perceived to be more closely identified with appropriate levels of teaching performance during their participation in the training program. Thus, these two studies suggest that training programs in specific departments can provide TAs with the skills necessary for discipline-specific instruction.

Training Focused on Specific Approaches. Of the studies we identified, two focused on the effects of specific kinds of TA training. Johnson (1987), after training TAs in the use of the Cognitive Interaction Analysis System, found that TAs increased their awareness of learners and made marked changes in their verbal behavior. He suggests that training in such analysis can enhance the flexibility of TAs. Andrews (1981) examined the interaction between teaching format and student style. The four TAs who participated in this study taught two sections of classes, each one with a peer-centered style and one with an instructor-centered style. As hypothesized, Andrews found an aptitude-treatment interaction in which self-described collaborative students reported more learning from the peer-centered format, while self-described competitive students reported more learning from the instructor-centered format. In addition, students with interpersonally oriented learning styles benefited more from interactive learning opportunities, such as quiz sections, but students with other learning styles gained more from impersonal media, such as textbooks.

The two studies in this category suggest specific approaches that could be considered for possible incorporation into a TA training program. Johnson's (1987) study suggests that the verbal behavior of TAs may be an area for focus in working to change TAs instructional behavior. Andrews's (1981) research suggests the importance not only of training TAs to use different instructional styles but also of alerting TAs to the importance of understanding how their instructional styles may interact with what their students bring to the classroom.

TAs' Characteristics and Student Ratings and Achievement

Thus far, we have focused on research investigating the components of TA training programs that can be manipulated by trainers. Other researchers have examined the relationship between various personal characteristics of TAs and TAs' effectiveness in the classroom. In these studies, the effectiveness of TAs is measured either through student ratings or through student achievement on examinations.

As summarized in Table 2, the studies we identified have examined only a few of TAs' characteristics in a few disciplines. Many of the characteristics of TAs shown in Table 2 cannot be manipulated by trainers or supervisors. Consequently, although these studies do not contain results that can be directly applied to TA training programs, they do suggest how TAs' characteristics may place constraints on the effectiveness of training programs. For example, in Bos, Zakrajsek, Wolf, and Stoll (1980), the TA's level of experience was positively related to the student's rating of knowledge, organization, and rapport. To the extent that levels of experience constrain how TAs may benefit from training, this characteristic will affect the outcomes of training and should be considered in the design of training strategies. The case study of Darling (1988) suggests that the socialization of new TAs is another factor that constrains the effectiveness of TA training (see Chapter Two of this volume).

Another way in which research on TAs' characteristics is relevant to training design is that it can suggest potential trait by training program interactions. For example, in Bos, Zakrajsek, Wolf, and Stoll (1980), prior degrees earned by TAs were related to student ratings of the TAs' knowledge, clarity, enthusiasm, organization, and preparation. Thus, the effectiveness of a TA training program may depend on the interaction between TAs' prior degrees or educational backgrounds and how TAs are trained.

Although the studies in Table 2 did not examine the effectiveness of TA training programs, trainers may be able to improve TAs' effectiveness by focusing on characteristics related to student ratings or academic performance. For example, in O'Hair and Babich (1981), TAs' awareness of affective components of classroom behavior was related to the ratings they had earned, suggesting that if part of a training program develops TAs' awareness of affective components in the classroom, TAs may be perceived as more effective. Chang, Berger, and Chang (1981) found that TAs' empathy was related to students' academic performance on multiple-choice and written exams. These results suggest that a TA training program that increases TAs' empathy with students may positively affect students' achievement.

Table 2. Studies Investigating Relationships of TAs' Characteristics and Student Outcomes

Reference	TAs/Disciplines	Explanatory Characteristics	Outcome Characteristics
Bos, Zakrajsek, Wolf, and Stoll (1980)	18 TAs Physical education	Gender; degree earned; teaching experience; undergraduate program; TA's experience, age	Student ratings; knowledge; organization; interaction; general evaluation
Chang, Berger, and Chang (1981)	12 TAs Psychology	TA's empathy; student's self-esteem	Exam scores; grade in class
Daniel (1983a)	60 TAs Varied departments (18)	Student (sex; grade level; course grade); TA (age; sex; SES; home state; parents' educational level)	Student ratings of communication effectiveness
Jacobs and Friedman (1988)	94 TAs Business and math	TA's nationality (foreign or native); class size; TA's teaching experience; student's expected grade	Student ratings on 22 items; final exam scores
Monts and Pickering (1981)	N not stated Chemistry	TA's experience; undergraduate school; TA's personal characteristics (age; sex; marital status)	Quantitative lab scores; exam scores
O'Hair and Babich (1981)	18 TAs Speech communication	TA's awareness of affective components of classroom behavior	Student ratings on 14 items
Pickering (1980)	20 TAs Chemistry	TA's prediction of students' grades	Exam performance
Tomita and McDowell (1981)	151 TAs Varied departments	Gender scale scores from Bem Sex Role Inventory (questionnaire)	Student ratings of TA's unwillingness to communicate; quality of content; quality of presentation

Student Ratings of TAs' Effectiveness

Research in this category has examined the underlying dimensions of student ratings of TAs (Braskamp, Caulley, and Costin, 1979; Daniel, 1983b). These studies identify the same underlying factors as studies of student ratings of faculty members (Abrami, 1985). Researchers have also examined the relationship of a TA's ratings to students' learning in class (Cohen, 1981; Hardy, 1983; Schweizer and Hardy, 1984). These results suggest a positive correlation between student ratings and student learning and are consistent with results for faculty members (Cohen, 1980; Marsh, 1987).

Other researchers have examined the relationship between students' evaluations, supervisors' evaluations, and self-evaluations of TAs (Brooks, Kelter, and Tipton, 1980). In this study, all such ratings were positively correlated. Again, these results are consistent with the results for faculty members (Marsh, 1987).

Conclusions and Future Directions for Research

Our analysis of the research on TAs, completed nearly a decade after the original work of Carroll (1980) and Levinson-Rose and Menges (1981), provides a number of insights that may be useful to those who work in TA training. The following comments highlight some of our conclusions and suggest future directions for research on TA training.

1. Empirical research on TA training is still lacking. Carroll (1980) suggested that there was a paucity of research that dealt specifically with training TAs. That deficiency still exists. We originally planned to report the results of our review in a meta-analysis and to make recommendations based on effect sizes, but we identified too few relevant studies to undertake such a procedure. Our review also discovered few case studies that employed modern qualitative approaches to examine TA training, and little research examining the generalizability of results across disciplines.

2. The research identified in this review suggests a number of directions for the future. One area for further study is the identification of programs that produce the greatest effects. When complex training programs are examined (as they were in many of the studies cited in this review), it is important to sort out the effects of various parts of the training programs in order to follow up on findings. For example, Bray and Howard (1980) suggest that a full training program—with seminars, videotaping, and feedback on midsemester ratings by students—did not provide effects significantly different from those for videotape feedback alone. Studies incorporating consultation with experts as part of a training program have suggested that consultation can be effective when it is focused on feedback that is based on student ratings and on videotapes. There is much room, however, for research that addresses how consultation can be conducted for the greatest impact on the instruction of TAs and, ultimately, on students' learning. The studies that have incorporated videotaping suggest that this is commonly a successful part of TA training programs. Nevertheless, there are many unanswered questions about specific ways for videotaping to be combined with consultation, to maximize its effects. Among the issues are the form of feedback (written or verbal), the amount of feedback, and the amount of positive or critical feedback that is appropriate.

Another area for further research is the importance of follow-up or ongoing training. Although Hendricson and others (1983) found that graduate students were able to show significant positive change even after one hundred days had elapsed between pre- and postvideotaping, other studies (Kanaga, 1979; Rodriguez, 1985) found that the effects of training did not last beyond the time of training.

Another direction for further research is evident in the Andrews (1981) study. Andrews's work suggests that the complexity of the teaching-learning act must be considered if TAs are to be appropriately prepared for instructional assignments. Part of such preparation will be an understanding of how complex student variables interact with approaches and styles that TAs are trained to use.

3. Research needs to employ methods that lead to more valid conclusions. To ground our theories in practice, we can employ thorough case studies to examine the contextual complexity within which TA training occurs. Empirical research that studies the effects of theoretically based TA training needs to be carried out, and meaningful measures of the degree of TA effectiveness need to be developed. Research designs that control for competing explanations of results also must be adopted. Studies of the generalizability of an intervention's effect over disciplines and university contexts will represent another step in the development of future research. All these approaches to research on TA training will strengthen its validity.

In recommending that the development of TA training approaches be informed by research results, we do not assume a simple model of research use that dictates a step-by-step way to examine relevant theories, define appropriate hypotheses, design studies, collect data, analyze results, and apply results to TA training. The ways in which research processes can affect training are undoubtedly recursive, with each part of the process calling on other parts. Clearly, theory development and inquiry can be grounded in actual practice and formative evaluation of training programs. Nevertheless, little systematic research is being conducted to determine how TAs can best be trained for their instructional responsibilities. It is clear from the research discussed in this review that TA training programs are being developed and modified without adequate attention to good research as a source of insights that can inform practice.

References

Abrami, P. C. "Dimensions of Effective College Instruction." *Review of Higher Education*, 1985, *8* (2), 211-238.

Andrews, J.D.W. "Teaching Format and Student Style: Their Interactive Effects on Learning." *Research in Higher Education*, 1981, *14* (2), 161-178.

Bingman, R. M. "Use of Student Evaluations to Improve Instruction." Paper presented at the annual forum of the Association for Institutional Research, Toronto, Ontario, May 1983.

Bos, R. R., Zakrajsek, D. B., Wolf, V., and Stoll, S. "Teaching Assistant Traits: Their Influence on Student Ratings." *Improving College and University Teaching*, 1980, *28* (2), 179-185.

Braskamp, L. A., Caulley, D., and Costin, F. "Student Ratings and Instructor Self-Ratings and Their Relationship to Student Achievement." *American Educational Research Journal*, 1979, *16* (3), 295-306.

Bray, J. H., and Howard, G. S. "Methodological Considerations in the Evaluation of a Teacher-Training Program." *Journal of Educational Psychology*, 1980, *72* (1), 62-70.

Brooks, D. W., Kelter, P. B., and Tipton, T. J. "Student Evaluation Versus Faculty Evaluation of Chemistry Teaching Assistants." *Journal of Chemical Education*, 1980, *57* (4), 294-295.

Carroll, J. G. "Effects of Training Programs for University Teaching Assistants: A Review of Empirical Research." *Journal of Higher Education*, 1980, *51* (2), 167-183.

Chang, A. F., Berger, S. E., and Chang, B. "The Relationship of Student Self-Esteem and Teacher Empathy to Classroom Learning." *Psychology, A Quarterly Journal of Human Behavior*, 1981, *18* (4), 21-24.

Cohen, P. A. "Effectiveness of Student-Rating Feedback for Improving College Instruction: A Meta-Analysis of Findings." *Research in Higher Education*, 1980, *13* (4), 321-341.

Cohen, P. A. "Student Ratings of Instruction and Student Achievement: A Meta-Analysis of Multisection Validity Studies." *Review of Educational Research*, 1981, *51* (3), 281-309.

Dalgaard, K. A. "Some Effects of Training on Teaching Effectiveness of Untrained University Teaching Assistants." *Research in Higher Education*, 1982, *17* (1), 39-50.

Daniel, A. "A Demographic Analysis of Students and Their GTA Instructors." Paper presented at the annual meeting of the Central States Speech Association, Lincoln, Nebraska, April 1983a.

Daniel, A. "Development of a Perceived Communication Effectiveness Scale." Paper presented at the annual meeting of the International Communication Association, Dallas, May 1983b.

Darling, A. L. "Graduate Student Socialization: Categories of Encounters." Paper presented at the annual meeting of the International Communication Association, New Orleans, May 1988.

Garner, L. C., Geitz, H., Knop, C., Magnan, S. S., and DiDonato, R. *Improved Training of Teaching Assistants Through Interdepartmental Cooperation*. Madison: University of Wisconsin, 1987.

Hardy, R. J. "The Role of Graduate Teaching Assistants in a Large American Government Class." *Teaching Political Science*, 1983, *10* (3), 136-140.

Hendricson, W. D., Hawkins, D. W., Littlefield, J. H., Kleffner, J. H., Hudepohl, N. C., and Herbert, R. "Effects of Providing Feedback to Lecturers Via Videotape Recordings and Observer Critiques." *American Journal of Pharmaceutical Education*, 1983, *47*, 239-244.

Jacobs, L. C., and Friedman, C. B. "Student Achievement Under Foreign Teaching Associates Compared with Native Teaching Associates." *Journal of Higher Education*, 1988, *59* (5), 551-563.

Johnson, G. R. "Changing the Behavior of Teachers." *The Journal of Staff, Program, and Organizational Development*, 1987, *5* (4), 155-158.

Kanaga, K. R. "The Evaluation of a Training Program for Undergraduate Teaching Assistants." Paper presented at the International Communication Association Conference, Philadelphia, May 1979.

Levinson-Rose, J., and Menges, R. J. "Improving College Teaching: A Critical Review of Research." *Review of Educational Research*, 1981, *51* (3), 403-434.

Liggett, S. L. "Learning to Grade Papers." Paper presented at the annual meeting of the Conference on College Composition and Communication, New Orleans, March 1986.

McKeachie, W. J., Lin, Y-G., Daugherty, M., Moffett, M. M., Neigler, C., Nork, J., Walz, M., and Baldwin, R. "Using Student Ratings and Consultation to Improve Instruction." *British Journal of Educational Psychology*, 1980, *50* (2), 168-174.

Marsh, H. W. "Students' Evaluations of University Teaching: Research Findings, Methodological Issues, and Directions for Future Research." *International Journal of Educational Research*, 1987, *11* (3), 253-388.

Monts, D. L., and Pickering, M. "Effects of TA Background on Student Laboratory Achievement."*Journal of Chemical Education*, 1981, *58* (10), 768-769.

Murray, H. G., and Smith, T. A. "Effects of Midterm Behavioral Feedback on End-of-Term Ratings of Instructor Effectiveness." Paper presented at the annual meeting of the American Educational Research Association, San Francisco, March 1989.

O'Hair, H. D., and Babich, R. M. "The Evaluation and Prediction of Affective Response to Graduate Teaching Assistants' Classroom Communication." Paper presented at the annual meeting of the Speech Communication Association, Anaheim, Calif., November 1981.

Pickering, M. "Teaching Assistant Predictions of Student Performance in General Chemistry." *Journal of Chemical Education*, 1980, *57* (5), 354-355.

Rodriguez, R. N. "Teaching Teaching to Teaching Assistants." *College Teaching*, 1985, *33* (4), 173-176.

Schweizer, S. L., and Hardy, R. J. "Analyzing Student Evaluations: Factors Affecting Teaching Performance Ratings." *Teaching Political Science*, 1984, *11* (3), 110-117.

Sharp, G. "Acquisition of Lecturing Skills by University Teaching Assistants: Some Effects of Interest, Topic Relevance, and Viewing a Model Videotape." *American Educational Research Journal*, 1981, *18* (4), 491-502.

Tomita, M., and McDowell, E. "Teaching Assistants' Perceptions of Formal and Informal Communications with Students." Paper presented at the annual meeting of the International Communication Association, Minneapolis, May 1981.

Robert D. Abbott is professor of educational psychology and director for program research at the Center for Instructional Development and Research, University of Washington.

Donald H. Wulff is assistant director of the Center for Instructional Development and Research, University of Washington.

C. Kati Szego is a Ph.D. student in systematic musicology and a staff consultant at the Center for Instructional Development and Research, University of Washington.

This chapter identifies resources useful for TA training, including print materials, videotapes, and program-development guides.

TA Training Resources

Delivee L. Wright

Resources in support of teaching assistant (TA) programs can provide enrichment and variety for the TA trainer or supervisor who is planning a program to respond to the needs of a particular department, college, or campus. Those described in this chapter represent a "snapshot" view of a constantly changing array of handbooks, videotapes, books, training strategies, program-development ideas, and other kinds of resources. With growing attention to TA training, refinements and additions will undoubtedly continue to evolve into an even more impressive range of choices. The purpose of this chapter is to describe the kinds of resources that have been useful to others and that may stimulate new ideas for planning effective programs.

Print Resources

Infinite possibilities exist for the print materials that might complement a TA training program. Budgetary considerations may dictate limitations, but it is important for TAs to have materials that can be used for future reference. The "teachable moment" for TAs may come long after the official program is completed.

Handouts. Articles, reprints, research summaries, "how-tos," diagrammatic models, checklists, resource lists, and policy statements are a few examples of useful handouts. One needs enough information to address a wide variety of needs and still keep the amount of new information from overwhelming the TA. Some programs provide a looseleaf notebook with dividers to help manage these handouts. These materials are the most easily adjusted to address the specific and timely needs of TAs.

Handbooks. Customized to fit particular sets of needs in a great many programs, handbooks allow a coherent sampling of materials, which can be related to the context of a specific campus. Typically, they are duplicated materials bound inexpensively. They often include a message from the administration, a table of contents, "how-to's," teaching suggestions, campus academic policies, guidelines for adapting to the TA role, bibliographies, campus resource lists, and other information. Handbooks can assist those who have not attended workshops, as well as those who have. Judging from the frequency of their use, one can say that handbooks are important resources, especially in programs that have been in operation long enough to provide a basis for selecting materials for inclusion. Bailey (1987) provides a detailed guide for designing these materials. Selected examples of these handbooks include the following.

Center for Instructional Development. *Now What? Readings on Surviving Your First Experience at College Teaching.* Syracuse, N.Y.: Syracuse University, 1987.

Center for Instructional Development and Research. *MENTOR.* (3rd ed.) Seattle: University of Washington, 1987.

Center for Teaching Effectiveness. *Handbook for Teaching Assistants.* Newark: University of Delaware, 1986.

The Graduate School. *Teaching Assistants' Handbook.* Evanston, Ill.: Northwestern University, 1983.

Office of Instructional Development. *Teaching Tips for TAs.* Los Angeles: University of California, 1987.

Office of Instructional Development and the Graduate School. *Handbook for Graduate Teaching Assistants.* Athens: University of Georgia, 1987.

Office of Instructional Resources. *Handbook for Teaching Assistants.* Champaign-Urbana: University of Illinois, 1980.

TA Training Program. *Teaching Assistance: A Handbook of Teaching Ideas.* San Diego: University of California, 1982.

TA Training Program. *The TA at UCLA: 1987-88 Handbook.* Los Angeles: University of California, 1988.

Teaching and Learning Center. *Instructional Resource Book for Teaching at UNL.* Lincoln: University of Nebraska, 1988.

University Teaching Program. *The Graduate Teacher Program Handbook.* Boulder: University of Colorado, 1988.

Books. Books that address college teaching can be a very helpful complement to a TA program. References of this kind should become part of every college teacher's personal collection. A TA program is the perfect setting to encourage this sort of reading. If budget constraints prohibit the purchase of books for TAs, a few copies in the bookstore or library are a good idea.

Axelrod, J. *The University Teacher as Artist: Toward an Aesthetics of Teaching with Emphasis on the Humanities.* San Francisco: Jossey-Bass, 1973.
Cahn, S. M. (ed.). *Scholars Who Teach: The Art of College Teaching.* Chicago: Nelson-Hall, 1973.
Chickering, A. W., and Associates. *The Modern American College: Responding to the New Realities of Diverse Students and a Changing Society.* San Francisco: Jossey-Bass, 1976.
Eble, K. E. *The Craft of Teaching: A Guide to Mastering the Professor's Art.* San Francisco: Jossey-Bass, 1976.
Eble, K. E. *The Aims of College Teaching.* San Francisco: Jossey-Bass, 1983.
Fuhrmann, B. S., and Grasha, A. F. *A Practical Handbook for College Teachers.* Boston: Little, Brown, 1983.
Gullette, M. M. (ed.). *The Art and Craft of Teaching.* Cambridge, Mass.: Harvard-Danforth Center for Teaching and Learning, 1982.
Katz, J., and Henry, M. *Turning Professors into Teachers: A New Approach to Faculty Development and Student Learning.* New York: Macmillan, 1988.
Lowman, J. *Mastering the Techniques of Teaching.* San Francisco: Jossey-Bass, 1984.
McKeachie, W. *Teaching Tips: A Guidebook for the Beginning College Teacher.* (8th ed.) Lexington, Mass.: Heath, 1986.
Menges, R. J., and Mathis, B. C. *Key Resources on Teaching, Learning, Curriculum, and Faculty Development: A Guide to the Higher Education Literature.* San Francisco: Jossey-Bass, 1988.
Meyers, C. *Teaching Students to Think Critically: A Guide for Faculty in All Disciplines.* San Francisco: Jossey-Bass, 1986.
Milton, O., and Associates. *On College Teaching: A Guide to Contemporary Practices.* San Francisco: Jossey-Bass, 1978.
Noonan, J. F. (ed.). *Learning About Teaching.* New Directions for Teaching and Learning, no. 4. San Francisco: Jossey-Bass, 1980.
Runkel, P., Harrison, R., and Runkel, M. (eds.). *The Changing College Classroom.* San Francisco: Jossey-Bass, 1972.
Travers, R.M.W., and Dillon, J. *The Making of a Teacher: A Plan for Professional Self-Development.* New York: Macmillan, 1975.

Bibliographies. Bibliographies, especially annotated ones, can identify much more comprehensive reading lists than handouts or handbooks can. In-depth readings can help create, over the long term, a college teacher who is knowledgeable about the choices one has in the classroom and who has developed a philosophical foundation for that role. TA programs tend to be limited in time and are targeted to avoid problems; they probably do not provide the breadth of issues that need to be addressed by career teachers. A bibliography provides a way to deal with this limitation.

Newsletters. Locally distributed newsletters generally contain teaching tips, announcements of workshops, deadlines, and other information pertinent to TAs. They provide relatively low-cost continuity in communication with TAs across the campus, in a way that takes very little of a busy TA's time. Border (1987) suggests ideas for making newsletters appealing to readers.

Manuals. Multisection manuals for courses taught by many TAs are sometimes provided by the department. Information is provided on timelines, grading policies, assignments, and successful teaching strategies. Such manuals are usually found in very large courses or in multisection courses.

Brochures. Brochures for students of TAs are designed to improve students' attitudes about having TAs as teachers. Vom Saal (1988) at the University of Missouri–Columbia includes information on how TAs are trained, what the advantages are of having a TA, what to do if things are not going well, and how students can facilitate classroom communication with both TAs and ITAs.

Audiovisual Resources

Access to well-maintained audiovisual equipment can be a determining factor in how such media are used for TA development. Most programs can incorporate materials that use transparencies, slides, audiotapes, films, and videotapes. Videotape recorders, cameras, and monitors are often used to provide individualized practice of skills. Some programs, such as those at the Harvard-Danforth Center and the University of Washington's Center for Instructional Development and Research, use studio classrooms, which are fitted with video production equipment for recorded teaching, or even transistorized earplugs, which allow coaching while a TA is teaching.

Technical production assistance can also make a big difference in the quality of the materials designed for use in a TA training program. Slides are relatively inexpensive, and transparencies can introduce color, image, and humor. Video is a very familiar mode of communication for most TAs. Videotapes can convey a message from a speaker, start discussions on TAs' problems or issues, compress time for a series of events, demonstrate positive models or negative ones, allow TAs to see themselves from students' point of view, record what has actually happened in a class for later analysis, and simulate any circumstance that a TA may face. All in all, video recordings provide a versatile and powerful instructional tool for TA programs.

It is relatively easy to produce videotapes locally, but many institutions have already produced them and made them available to others for a nominal charge. Examples include the following.

Center for Instructional Development and Research, University of Washington.
- "Encounters with Teaching," with guide. Thought-provoking questions about enactments of difficult classroom situations. (27 min.)
- "The Role of the Graduate Teaching Assistant." Concerns TAs' responsibilities.

Center for Instructional Development, Syracuse University. "Dealing with Problems," with leader's guide. Vignettes to stimulate discussion about difficult situations.

Media Resource Center, Iowa State University. "Teaching Assistant Communication Strategies." Three tapes with vignettes to stimulate discussion on eight teaching skills.

Center for English as a Second Language, University of Arizona. "The University Lecture." Enactment of four lecture styles, including good and bad examples.

The Learning Shop, Glenview, Ill. "The Instructor's Shop." Hints and techniques for first-time instructors.

Office of Instructional Development, University of California, Los Angeles. "Mastery Teaching Tapes."

Center for Teaching Professions, Northwestern University. "College Classroom Vignettes." A survey of typical classroom situations.

Extension Instructor Development, University of California, Los Angeles. "Instructor Development Videotapes."
- "There's More to It Than Teaching." Discussion stimulators for four situations that new instructors face. (14 min.)
- "Making the Lecture Come Alive." Ways to combine instructional skills with personal style. (24 min.)
- "Designing Instructor Orientation Programs." Specific insights into working with adult students. (22 min.)

Office of Instructional Consultation, University of California, Santa Barbara.
- "Issues on Campus: A View from the Lab." A documentary spoof of students caught in behavior that TAs will encounter. (23 min.)
- "Discipline-Specific Series."
   1. Chemistry: "Elements of Teaching, Part I: Basic Teaching Skills." Skills for lab discussion. (13 min.)
   2. Chemistry: "Elements of Teaching, Part II: Interacting with Students." Ways to enhance TA–student interaction. (8 min.)
   3. Engineering: "Instructional Techniques for Engineering TAs." Illustrates eight teaching skills. (18 min.)

4. Math: "Problem Solving in Mathematics." Ways to promote students' participation in problem solving. (13 min.)
   5. Physics: "Getting Past Those First-Quarter Blues." Emphasizes active involvement. (15 min.)
   6. Physics: "Approaches to Problem Solving: The Good and Bad." Examples, with analysis. (26 min.)

Other Resources for TA Programs

The design of a good TA training program goes beyond questions of who will participate and what materials will be used. Processes used for program development should be carefully selected to achieve the desired outcomes.

Program design always begins with a careful needs assessment. Tools for this may include interviews of students, TAs, supervisors, or chairs; observations of the kinds of teaching duties and tasks that TAs perform; surveys of opinions and attitudes related to the TA role; exit interviews of TAs to gather their perceptions of need; and collection of data on numbers and types of responsibilities.

Evaluation can identify needed modifications to a program. Tools may include feedback questionnaires for TAs; interviews with departmental chairs or supervisors; feedback from students of TAs; observation of teaching behaviors; videotapes of classroom teaching, using observation instruments keyed to program goals; and examination of unobtrusive indicators, such as grades given, students' dropout rates, and so forth.

The following paragraphs highlight some TA training program considerations. A timetable for coordination of planning deadlines, communications, and task accomplishment is an important tool. The coordinator must orchestrate this timetable with detailed care, to bring all elements together efficiently. In addition to the timetable, mechanisms for record keeping and reporting on participation provide data for future training decisions.

Instructional strategies are selected according to the kinds of activities that will enable TAs to function well as teachers. Large groups with speakers can provide informational or inspirational messages. Small groups may be preferable for developing skills, adjusting attitudes, and identifying individual concerns. Panel presentations by faculty members or experienced TAs can address different approaches to an issue or a problem. Typical problems can be handled with case studies, simulations, or role playing. Perhaps the most powerful strategy for improving teaching behavior is microteaching. This is a short practice session with a limited topic, and it is usually videotaped. Playback and analysis precede reteaching, in which suggestions for improvement are incorporated.

Program format depends largely on local calendars and traditions, as well as on the availability of participants and resources. Typically, presemester workshops of one to five days are planned. Campuswide programs may include time to meet with departmental supervisors about more targeted expectations.

Some programs have shorter, presemester workshops, followed by weekly or monthly instructional sessions. A traditional class for credit is another approach to preparing TAs for college teaching. Still another approach is to provide individual consultation to TAs. This assistance can be provided by supervising faculty members, TA program staff members, or other experienced TAs.

Recognition includes a variety of approaches. Stipends for program participation are occasionally provided, but certificates of participation are more common. Awards have also been established to encourage outstanding classroom performance by TAs.

The following sources contain ideas useful for program design.

Andrews, J.D.W. (ed.). *Strengthening the Teaching Assistant Faculty.* New Directions for Teaching and Learning, no. 22. San Francisco: Jossey-Bass, 1985.

Bergquist, W. H., and Phillips, S. R. *A Handbook for Faculty Development.* Vols. 1-3. Washington, D.C.: Council of Independent Colleges, 1975-1981.

Blizzard, A. C., Hogan, R. C., and Roy, D. E. *Developing a Departmental Program for Teaching Assistants: A Manual.* Hamilton, Ontario, Canada: Instructional Development Center, McMaster University, 1981.

Chism, N. (ed.). *Employment and Education of Teaching Assistants: Readings from a National Conference.* Columbus: Center for Teaching Excellence, Ohio State University, 1987.

Eison, J., Bonwell, C., Renegar, S., and Summary, R. *Teaching Effectiveness Workshop.* Cape Girardeau, Missouri: Center for Teaching and Learning, 1987.

Lewis, K., and Povlacs, J. (eds.). *Face to Face: A Sourcebook of Individual Consultation Techniques for Faculty/Instructional Developers.* Stillwater, Okla.: New Forums Press, 1988.

Unruh, D. *Teaching Assistant Training: A Guide for Developing Departmental TA Training Programs.* Los Angeles: Office of Instructional Development, University of California, 1987.

Wadsworth, E. (ed.). *A Handbook of New Practitioners.* Stillwater, Okla.: New Forums Press, 1988.

Wood, L. *Sourcebook for Developing TA Training Programs.* Berkeley: Teaching and Evaluation Services, University of California, 1978.

Conferences and Clearinghouses for Resources

The Professional and Organizational Development Network in Higher Education (c/o Teaching and Learning Center, 121 Benton Hall,

University of Nebraska, Lincoln, Nebraska 68588-0623) sponsors an annual national conference, as well as publications that often have content useful for the development of TA programs. It also provides networking opportunities for TA program coordinators.

The Second National Conference on the Training and Employment of Teaching Assistants (hosted by the Center for Instructional Development and Research, University of Washington, Seattle, November 15-18, 1989) is another rich resource for program-development information.

Discipline-centered teaching journals and conferences also provide some references for the education of TAs. Subscription information can be found in the Source Journal Index of the *Current Index to Journals in Education* (Oryx Press).

At the 1986 national conference on the Employment and Education of Teaching Assistants (Columbus, Ohio), plans were made to establish clearinghouses for information related to the education of TAs. The National Clearinghouse for Teaching Assistants was established through the ERIC collection, and the International Teaching Assistant Material Collection was established with Janet Constantinides at the University of Wyoming.

Since TA training programs require current, inexpensive, and easily accessible resources to support training efforts, institutionally prepared materials may continue to dominate the resources collections. Many of the resources identified in this chapter have been used by numerous institutions as models to be adapted or used directly with TAs. One of the best ways to locate such TA training materials is through the national clearinghouses. Because the clearinghouses have only recently been established, however, it may take some time before all materials on TA training are readily available.

References

Bailey, J. G. "TA Handbooks: What Should They Include?" In N. Chism (ed.), *Employment and Education of Teaching Assistants: Readings from a National Conference.* Columbus: Center for Teaching Excellence, Ohio State University, 1987.

Border, L. "Producing a TA Newsletter." In N. Chism (ed.), *Employment and Education of Teaching Assistants: Readings from a National Conference.* Columbus: Center for Teaching Excellence, Ohio State University, 1987.

vom Saal, D. *Teaching Assistants at Mizzou.* Columbia: TA Training and Development Program, University of Missouri, 1988.

Delivee L. Wright is director of the Teaching and Learning Center, University of Nebraska–Lincoln, and executive director for administration of the Professional and Organizational Development Network in Higher Education.

Index

A

Abbott, R. D., 2, 3, 7, 14, 111, 124
Abraham, R. G., 81, 86
Abrami, P. C., 120, 122
Active learning strategies, 12; models of, 91-94; resistance to, 95-96; small-group discussion as a basis of, 89-90, 93-96; writing as a basis of, 89, 91-93, 95, 96
Allen, V. L., 16, 22
American Association of Higher Education, 8
American Council on Education, 101
Anderson, J. A., 31, 35
Andrews, J.D.W., 8, 13, 114, 117, 121, 122, 131
Angelo, T. A., 2, 99, 103, 107, 108
Arizona, University of, 129
Assessment, of students' learning, 101-104, 107
Assessment, of teaching assistants. *See* Evaluation, of teaching assistants
Association of American Colleges, 100, 107
Astin, A., 24, 35
Audiovisual resources, for teacher assistant training, 128-130. *See also* Videotaping
Axelrod, J., 127

B

Babich, R. M., 118, 123
Bailey, J. G., 126, 132
Baldwin, R., 123
Banks, J. A., 28, 35
Bates, A. P., 18, 22
Bauer, G., 2, 57, 70
Belenky, M., 31, 34, 35
Berger, C. R., 19, 21
Berger, S. E., 118, 119, 122
Bergquist, W. H., 131
Bias, in instructional materials, 34
Bingman, R. M., 113, 114, 122
Blanchard, K., 45, 53

Blegen, T. C., 101, 107
Blizzard, A. C., 131
Boehrer, J., 15, 19, 21, 101, 107
Bonwell, C., 131
Book, C. L., 43, 52
Books, for teaching assistant training, 126-127. *See also* Handbooks, for teaching assistant training
Border, L., 128, 132
Bos, R. R., 118, 122
Braskamp, L. A., 120, 122
Bray, J. H., 113, 114, 120, 122
Brooks, D. W., 120, 122
Brown University, 68
Byrd, P., 74, 76, 83, 85, 86

C

Cahn, S. M., 127
California, University of, at Berkeley, 101
California, University of, at Davis (UCD), 60-61, 65, 68
California, University of, at Los Angeles, 60, 68, 126, 129
California, University of, at San Diego, 68, 69, 126
California, University of, at Santa Barbara, 129
Cano, J., 1, 23, 36
Carroll, J. G., 111, 112, 120, 122
Caulley, D., 120, 122
Chang, A. F., 118, 119, 122
Chang, B., 118, 119, 122
Chicago, University of, 8
Chickering, A. W., 32, 35, 127
Chism, N.V.N., 1, 23, 36, 131
Cognitive intervention analysis system, 115, 117
Cohen, P. A., 120, 122
Classroom research, as approach to teaching assistant development, 106-107; classroom assessment as part of, 103-104; for teaching assistant evaluation, 99-102, 105
Client-consultant models, 82, 105-106

Colleagues in training, teaching assistants as, 44, 47-50
Colorado, University of, 60, 69, 126
Communication: cross-cultural, 72-73, 75, 83; and socialization, 20-21
Constantinides, J. C., 2, 71, 72, 74, 76, 77, 83, 86, 132
Constantino, M., 2, 79, 86
Cooper, R. M., 101, 107
Cornell University, 69
Costin, F., 120, 122
Council of Graduate Schools, 8
Cross, K. P., 2, 99, 103, 107, 108
Cross-cultural communication, 72-73, 75, 83
Crumpbacker, L., 26, 35
Cultural socialization, of teaching assistants, 17
Current Index to Journals in Education, 132

D

Dalgaard, K. A., 113, 114, 122
Daniel, A., 119, 120, 122
Darling, A. L., 1, 15, 16, 18, 19, 20, 21, 22, 118, 122
Daugherty, M., 123
Delaware, University of, 126
DiDonato, R., 122
Dillon, J., 127
Disabled students, 23-24, 26, 29, 32, 34
Discipline-specific instruction, 85, 116-117
Diverse student body, teaching of, 23-35, 84

E

Eble, K. E., 127
Educational Research and Information Center (ERIC), 112, 132
Educational role models. See Professorial role models
Eisenberg, E. M., 43, 52
Eison, J., 131
Ethnic minority students, 23-25, 28-31, 34, 84. See also Diverse student body, teaching of
Evaluation, of teaching assistants, 41, 47, 49, 65, 105; resources for, 130; through training programs, 59, 65, 112-116, 120-121

F

Farris, C. R., 2, 89, 97
Feedback. See Evaluation, of teaching assistants
Fisher, M., 71, 77
Friedman, C. B., 119, 123
Fuhrmann, B. S., 127
Fuller, F. F., 43, 53

G

Garner, L. C., 114, 116, 122
Gay/lesbian students, 23, 26-27, 29, 30, 34. See also Diverse student body, teaching of
Geitz, H., 122
Georgia, University of, 126
Georgia State University, 81
Grasha, A. F., 127
Green, M. F., 9, 13, 23, 35
Gullette, M. M., 127

H

Hall, R. M., 26, 35
Hammill, D., 26, 35
Handbooks, for teaching assistant training, 66, 126. See also Books, for teaching assistant training
Hardy, R. J., 120, 122, 123
Harrison, R., 127
Harvard University, 69
Harvard-Danforth Center, 128
Hatch, D. H., 2, 89, 97
Hawkins, D. W., 122
Hendricson, W. D., 113, 114, 121, 122
Henry, M., 106, 107, 127
Herbert, R., 122
Hersey, P., 45, 53
Hilliard, A. G., 31, 35
Hogan, R. C., 131
Holley, J. W., 18, 22
Howard, G. S., 113, 114, 120, 122
Hudepohl, N. C., 122
Hymes, D., 84, 86

I

Illinois, University of, 65, 69, 126
Information-seeking strategies, 19, 20
Instructional/faculty development units, 58-60, 62, 66, 68, 73, 83

Instructor-centered teaching approach, 114, 117
International Teaching Assistant Material Collection, 132
International teaching assistants (ITAs), 2; cross-cultural communications for, 72-73, 75, 83; instructional development for, 83; languages assessment/training for, 72-74, 80-81, 83; and minority undergraduates, 84; orientation of, 71, 72, 82; roles of, 79-80; training of, 66-67, 71-76, 79-85
Iowa State University, 81, 129

J

Jacobs, L. C., 119, 123
Joblin, F. M., 18, 22
Johnson, G. R., 115, 117, 123
Junior colleagues, teaching assistants as, 44, 45, 47, 50

K

Kagan, D. M., 43, 53
Kanaga, K. R., 115, 117, 121, 123
Katz, J., 106, 107, 127
Kelter, P. B., 120, 122
Kendall, P., 16, 22
Kleffner, J. H., 122
Knop, C., 122
Kuroiwa, P., 31, 35

L

Laing, G. J., 8, 13
Larson, S., 26, 35
Learning disabilities, 10, 26
Learning styles, 10, 12, 31-33, 117
Leigh, J., 26, 35
Levinson-Rose, J., 111, 112, 120, 123
Lewis, K., 131
Liggett, S. L., 115, 116, 117, 123
Lin, Y-G., 123
Littlefield, J. H., 122
Louis, M. R., 17, 22
Lowman, J., 127

M

McDowell, E., 119, 123
McKeachie, W. J., 112, 113, 115, 123, 127

McNutt, G., 26, 35
Magnon, S. S., 122
Marienau, C., 32, 35
Marsh, H. W., 120, 123
Mathis, B. C., 127
Menges, R. J., 111, 112, 120, 123, 127
Mentorship, 43, 45, 50, 104-106
Merton, R., 16, 22
Meyers, C., 127
Michigan, University of, 62, 69, 85
Michigan State University, 62, 81
Microteaching, 51, 59, 65, 81, 115-116, 130
Milton, O., 127
Minigrant programs, 66
Minority students. *See* Diverse student body, teaching of
Missouri, University of, 62, 67, 69, 83, 128
Moffett, M. M., 123
Monts, D. L., 119, 123
Murray, H. G., 113, 115, 123

N

National Clearinghouse for Teaching Assistants, 132
National Conference on the Training and Employment of Teaching Assistants, 132
Nebraska, University of, 126, 132
Neigler, C., 123
Nontraditional students, 23, 84; course design for, 30-31; encouraging class participation of, 29-30; preparation for teaching of, 33-34; prevention of discrimination against, 29; providing feedback to, 32; treatment of, as individuals, 28-29; various learning styles of, 31-33
Noonan, J. F., 127
Nork, J., 123
Northwestern University, 126, 129
Nyquist, J. D., 1, 2, 3, 7, 13, 14, 37, 50, 53

O

O'Hair, H. D., 118, 119, 123
Ohio State University, 61, 69, 81, 85
Older students. *See* Returning adult students

P

Pavalko, R. M., 18, 22
Pedagogy, 59, 72, 74, 84
Peer-centered teaching approach, 114, 117
Peer relations, of teaching assistants, 10, 18, 21, 47, 49, 106
Pemberton, G., 24, 35
Pennsylvania State University, The, 81
Phillips, S. R., 131
Pickering, M., 119, 123
Plakans, B. S., 81, 86
Povlacs, J., 131
Professional and Organizational Development Network in Higher Education, 131
Professorial role models, 41–43, 45, 48
Professors, quality of, for future, 12, 99–101
Professors, quantity of, for future, 8–9, 43, 99–100
Program design: for international teaching assistants, 82; resources for, 130–131; during teaching assistant developmental stages, 47
Proseminars, 47, 49, 51
Pruitt, A. S., 1, 23, 36

R

Reader, G., 16, 22
Renegar, S., 131
Research: future directions for, 120–121; on student ratings of teaching assistants' effectiveness, 120; on teaching assistants' personal characteristics and teaching effectiveness, 118–120; on teaching assistant training methods, 111–118
Resources, for teaching assistant training, 66; audiovisual, 128–130; conferences as, 8, 131–132; informational clearinghouses as, 132; print, 125–128
Returning adult students, 23–26, 29, 32, 34
Rodriguez, R. N., 115, 116, 121, 123
Role socialization, of teaching assistants, 16–17
Rosen, B. C., 18, 22
Rounds, P. L., 83, 85, 86
Roy, D. E., 131
Runkel, M., 127
Runkel, P., 127

S

Sandler, B. R., 26, 35
Sarbin, T. R., 16, 22
Sarkisian, E., 15, 19, 21, 101, 107
Schön, D. A., 50, 53
Schweizer, S. L., 120, 123
Sedlacek, W. E., 24, 35
Seldin, P., 53
Senior learners, teaching assistants as, 44, 46, 47
Sequeira, D-L., 2, 79, 85, 86
Sharp, G., 115, 116, 123
Shulman, L. S., 42, 53
Small-group discussion, as an active learning strategy, 89–90, 93–96
Small-group instructional diagnosis (SGID), 66
Smith, R., 76, 77
Smith, T. A., 113, 115, 123
Social support system. *See* Peer relations, of teaching assistants
Socialization, of teaching assistants, 15, 118; and changing roles, 16–17; through communication strategies, 17–21
Southern Illinois University, 81
Speaking Proficiency English Assessment Kit (SPEAK), 80
Sprague, J., 1, 37, 53
Staton, A. Q., 1, 15, 16, 18, 22
Staton-Spicer, A. Q., 16, 18, 22
Stearns, J., 10, 13, 40, 53
Stoll, S., 118, 122
Stoltenberg, C., 43, 53
Student ratings, of teaching assistants, 112–115, 118–120
Student-centered teaching, 29–30
Summary, R., 131
Supervision, of teaching assistants: during developmental stages, 45–50; ideal scenario for, 51–52
Supervisors, of teaching assistants: as employment managers, 38–41, 45, 48, 50; as mentors, 43, 45, 50; as professorial role models, 41–43, 45, 48, 50

Svinicki, M. D., 2, 57, 70
Swales, J., 83, 86
Syracuse University, 62, 64, 66, 67, 69, 126, 129
Szego, C. K., 2, 111, 124

T

Teaching assistants (TAs), 1-3; and active learning strategies, 12, 89-97; and adapting to rules and procedures, 19; and classroom research, 99-107; developmental stages of, 43-45; duties of, 7, 46-48, 50; evaluation of, 41, 47, 49, 65, 112-116, 120-121, 130; international, 2, 66-67, 71-76, 79-85; orientation of, 20, 51, 62, 63, 65, 116; and peer relationships, 10, 18, 21, 47, 49, 106; socialization of, 15-21; supervision of, 37-52; and teaching a diverse student body, 9-10, 23-35; training of, 7-13, 49, 51, 57-69, 104-107, 111-121, 125-132
Teaching Goals Inventory, 103
Teaching methods. *See* Learning styles
Test of English as a Foreign Language (TOEFL), 80
Test of Spoken English, (TSE), 80
Tipton, T. J., 120, 122
Tomita, M., 119, 123
Training, of international teaching assistants, 71, 79-81; curriculum for, 83-84; discipline-specific approach to, 85; program design for, 82; staffing for, 83; success of, 75-76; various programs for, 72-74
Training, of teaching assistants: approaches to, 104-106; current programs for, 68-69; departmental responsibilities in, 51, 58-61; evaluation of, 67-68; follow-up activities in, 64-66; program design for, 57-69, 131; remuneration for, 62; research on, 111-121; resources for, 66, 125-132; videotaping, 59, 65-66, 120-121, 128, 130
Travers, R.M.W., 127

U

U.C. Berkeley Classroom Research Project, 101-102, 103
Undergraduate students, emphasis on quality education for, 10, 13, 84-85
Unruh, D., 131

V

Vander Haegen, E., 26, 35
Videotaping: for evaluation of teaching assistants, 49, 105; for training international teaching assistants, 81-82; for training teaching assistants, 59, 65-66, 113-116, 120-121, 128-130
vom Saal, D. R., 73, 76, 77, 83, 86, 128, 132

W

Wadsworth, E., 131
Walz, M., 123
Washington, University of, 61, 65, 69, 84, 85, 126, 128, 129, 132
Weimer, M., 2, 57, 70
Williams, J. M., 43, 53
Wilson, T., 10, 13, 40, 53
Wise, W. M., 8, 13
Wolf, V., 118, 122
Wolocowitz, J., 73, 77
Women students, 23-24, 26-30, 31, 34
Wood, L., 131
Wright, D. L., 2, 125, 132
Writing, as an active learning strategy, 89, 91-93, 95, 96
Wulff, D. H., 2, 3, 7, 13, 14, 50, 53, 111, 124
Wyoming, University of, 62, 69, 75, 76, 81, 132

Z

Zakrajsek, D. B., 118, 122
Zeichner, K. M., 16, 22

F. S. Weaver, (ed.). *Promoting Inquiry in Undergraduate Learning.*
New Directions for Teaching and Learning, no. 38. San Francisco: Jossey-Bass, Summer 1989.

ERRATUM

Page 36, lines 42-43 and page 37, line 1:

This sentence should read as follows: While the course's basic intentions and structure have remained intact, we have made substantial changes in the readings and presentations in response to students' suggestions.